THE NEWCOMERS SERIES

HISPANICS IN U.S. HISTORY

THROUGH 1865

VOLUME 1

GLOBE BOOK COMPANY
Englewood Cliffs, N.J.

Front cover, clockwise: Sor Juana Inés de la Cruz, Hernando de Soto, David Farragut, María Josefa Ortiz de Domínguez
Cover art: David Dircks
Design: Function Thru Form, Inc.
Photo research: Omni-Photo Communication, Inc.

Printed in the United States of America
10 9 8 7 6 5 4 3
ISBN 1-55675-588-0

Globe Book Company
A division of Simon & Schuster
Englewood Cliffs, New Jersey 07632

CONTENTS

Chapter 1 SPAIN AND THE NEW WORLD

To the student: The notes printed in green in Chapter 1 will help you get started on Hispanics in American History, Volume 1.

AIM: How did Spain become a leader in exploring the New World?

Read the text to answer the AIM question(s).

1. Great changes were taking place in Europe during the 1400s. During this time, a Muslim empire in the Middle East controlled the spice and silk trade in Asia. The Europeans wanted to buy these spices and silks. So, European merchants and sailors tried to find water routes to Asia. This led Europeans to improve their ships and to invent better sailing instruments.

2. Spain was one of the European countries that was experiencing change. The land that is now Spain was divided into four kingdoms called Castile, Granada, Aragon, and Navarre. In 1469, Ferdinand, the prince of Aragon, married Isabella, the princess of Castile. Ten years later their kingdoms became united under one rule. By 1492, they had conquered Granada. In 1512, the union of Spain was completed by seizing the kingdom of Navarre.

3. Meanwhile, an Italian named Christopher Columbus believed that there was an easy way to reach Asia from Europe. He wanted to sail west in the hope that he would

The first sentence in each paragraph gives the main idea.

▲ Christopher Columbus called himself Cristóbal Colón and wrote all his journals and letters in Spanish or Latin.

The caption will help you understand the illustration.

find a shorter route to Asia. A shorter route would improve trade between the two continents. Columbus's biggest problem was that he did not have enough money to fund the trip.

4. In 1484, Columbus decided to try to get support for his plan from King Ferdinand and Queen Isabella of Spain. He met them for the first time in 1486, but they could not pay much attention to Columbus's plan at the time. Spain was at war with Granada. Finally, in 1492, Ferdinand and Isabella saw Columbus and gave him part of the money for his plan. With that money, and some more that he borrowed, Columbus bought three small ships, the *Niña*, the *Pinta*, and the *Santa María*. The money also paid for supplies and sailors.

5. Columbus set sail on his first voyage in August 1492. On October 12, a sailor on the *Pinta*, named Rodrigo de Triana, sighted land. Columbus and his sailors landed on the island of Guanahaní, which Columbus renamed San Salvador. Columbus sailed on to the islands of Cuba and Hispaniola. He did see some gold worn by the people living on the islands. However, he did not find the spices, silk, and other riches of the East. He hoped that he would find these goods on his next voyage.

6. Columbus received a hero's welcome back in Spain. News of his discoveries traveled fast throughout Europe. Ferdinand and Isabella honored Columbus. They had already given him the title Admiral of the Ocean Sea and made him governor-general of all the land he might discover.

7. Columbus made three other trips to what became known as the **New World.** On his second trip in 1493, he had 17 ships and about 1,500 people. Many of these people were brought to settle the new land and establish trade. In all his trips Columbus never found Asia, or great riches of gold, silk, and spices. Instead he had reached islands in the Caribbean Sea and the coasts of what were to be called Central and South America. Columbus's voyages opened the door for Spain to claim large empires in the New World.

Vocabulary words are defined in context nearby, and are also found in the Glossary.

Study Tip to review, reread the first sentence in each paragraph. Also review the time chart on the back cover.

Understanding What You Have Read

Check your comprehension by doing these activities.

A. Choose each correct answer and write the letter in the space provided.

_____ 1. The Europeans were interested in finding a water route to Asia because they wanted to
   a. travel.
   b. conquer foreign lands.
   c. buy spice and silk.

_____ 2. In 1479, Ferdinand and Isabella united
   a. Granada and Navarre.
   b. Navarre and Aragon.
   c. Aragon and Castile.

_____ 3. When Columbus returned to Spain after his first voyage, he was
   a. punished for not finding Asia.
   b. honored as a hero.
   c. told his discovery was not important.

_____ 4. The main idea of *paragraph 4* is that
   a. Columbus did not discover new land.
   b. Columbus wanted to sail west from Europe to Asia.
   c. Isabella and Ferdinand helped Columbus by supplying money for his voyage.

B. In each of the sentences that follow, the underlined word or words make the sentence true or false. If the sentence is true, write **T** in the blank. If it is false, write the word or words that would make the sentence true.

_____ 1. Columbus first went to Ferdinand and Isabella in the <u>1460s</u>.

_____ 2. In 1492, Columbus's plan was <u>rejected</u> by Isabella and Ferdinand.

_____ 3. On his second voyage, Columbus had <u>three</u> ships.

_____ 4. Columbus had not reached <u>Asia</u>.

Each chapter has one of these activities: **Building Geography Skills, Linking Past to Present,** or **Daily Life.**

Building Geography Skills

Study the map. Then answer the questions.

1. On which voyage did Columbus reach Puerto Rico? _____

2. On which voyage did Columbus first visit the north coast of Cuba? _____

3. On which voyage did Columbus reach Trinidad and the coast of Venezuela? _____

_____

4. List at least three of the places Columbus visited on his fourth and final voyage.

_____

_____

_____

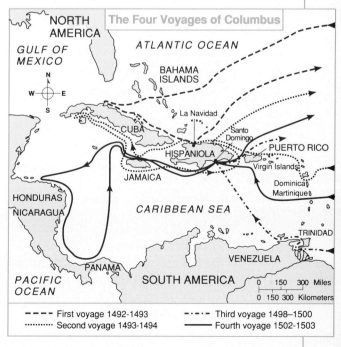

3 ▶

Spotlight on People

▲ Isabella listens to Columbus's plan to sail west to Asia.

Isabella I of Castile. At the age of 18, Isabella of Castile showed her strong-willed nature. She defied her older brother, the king of Castile. Without her brother's approval, Isabella married Ferdinand of Aragon in 1469.

By the time she was 28, Isabella was queen of both Castile and Aragon. Castile, however, remained under Isabella's direct rule. Because of her powerful position, Isabella was able to promote art and literature. She kept a tight control over the Roman Catholic church in Castile. She also ordered the Jews and Muslims to become Christians or leave.

Without Isabella's support and influence, it is possible that Columbus might never have discovered the Americas. She agreed to provide him with about two-thirds of the money he needed for his project. She also agreed to let him have ten percent of the profits from business conducted in lands under his control. In return, Columbus had to claim the lands he discovered for Castile.

Another major concern Isabella had was the conversion of Native Americans to Christianity. She strongly believed in her Roman Catholic faith. She felt that if the Native Americans were to come under her rule, they should learn the religion of her nation.

Isabella died a few days after Columbus returned from his last voyage in 1504. As a result of Isabella's decision to support Columbus, Spain would soon make claim to millions of square miles of the New World.

Recalling the Facts

Choose each correct answer and write the letter in the space provided.

_____ 1. After Isabella married Ferdinand, Castile was ruled by
  a. Ferdinand.
  b. both Isabella and Ferdinand.
  c. Isabella.

_____ 2. Isabella felt strongly that Castile should be
  a. Christian. b. Jewish. c. Muslim.

_____ 3. Isabella provided Columbus with
  a. all her jewels.
  b. about two-thirds of the money he needed for his project.
  c. no money, but with promises of the title of admiral.

_____ 4. Isabella favored the
  a. conversion of Native Americans to Christianity.
  b. ending of any rights for Native Americans.
  c. return of all lands in the New World to the Native Americans.

The Arts and Technology

▲ The *Santa María* was the largest of the three small ships.

The Santa María. The *Santa María* was a kind of ship called a **nao**. It was larger than Columbus's other two ships and had a deck in the middle. It had three masts and was about 117 feet (36 meters) long. His other ships were less than half the *Santa María*'s size. They were **caravels**. These ships had three masts and no deck in the middle. In the 1400s, caravels were the best made ships in Europe.

On his first voyage, Columbus commanded the *Santa María* himself. It was his flagship.

On Christmas Day, 1492, however, it was wrecked near Hispaniola. Columbus and his men used the wood from the ship to build a fort, La Navidad. Columbus left some men to start a colony and returned to Spain on the *Niña*.

1. Why was the *Santa María* a good kind of ship for Columbus? _____

_____

2. What became of the *Santa María*? _____

_____

Critical Thinking helps you think about what you have read and puts the chapter into historical perspective.

CHAPTER REVIEW: CRITICAL THINKING

Christopher Columbus was not the only sailor to believe that it was possible to sail west and find land. Yet he was the first to do so and return to Europe with the news. Columbus had kept asking different rulers for help until someone agreed to supply him with money for ships. For example, he asked the king of Portugal in 1484 and was rejected. **Support your opinion.**

1. What difference might there be in history if the king of Portugal had agreed to give ships to

   Columbus in 1484? _____

   _____

2. Why was it important that Columbus continued to follow his dream after he had been

   turned down several times? _____

   _____

Chapter 2 SPANISH EXPLORERS IN NORTH AMERICA

AIM: Who were some of the early Spanish explorers in North America? What areas, now part of the United States, did they reach and map between 1513 and 1543?

1. Once the Spanish people had heard about the New World, many of them wanted to go there. The Spanish explorers were called **conquistadores,** which means "conquerors." Most went as fortune hunters. Roman Catholic missionaries also went. The missionaries wanted to spread their religion to peoples of the New World.

2. Juan Ponce de León, who had been with Columbus on his second voyage, explored America on his own. In 1508, he found some gold on the island now known as Puerto Rico. He claimed that island for Spain. In 1513, he discovered the beautiful land of Florida and claimed that for Spain also. Ponce de León was probably the first European to land on what is now known as the United States.

3. Other Spanish explorers carried on the explorations. In 1519, Alonso Alvarez de Piñeda sailed into the Gulf of Mexico and mapped the coastal area. He was the first European to reach the Mississippi River. A few years later Esteban Gómez explored the east coast of North America from Florida to Nova Scotia.

4. In 1527, another Spanish explorer, Pánfilo de Narváez, explored territory in and around Florida. He had heard of gold to the north of Florida and marched his men inland. When they returned to the coast, they discovered that their ships were gone. They tried to sail along the coast of the Gulf of Mexico in makeshift boats. Most of the men died.

5. In 1539 Estevanico, a Black slave and survivor of Narváez's expedition, explored Arizona and New Mexico. Estevanico was killed, but his companion, Father Marcos de Niza, survived and told about the new lands. About the same time, another Spanish explorer explored the southeastern part of the United States. His name was Hernando de Soto. These explorers searched for, but never found, great riches such as gold.

6. In 1540, Francisco Vásquez de Coronado explored and claimed the southwest region of what is now the United States for Spain. He had heard about the "Seven Cities of Gold" from Father Marcos de Niza. He never found those golden cities. His men, however, did reach the Grand Canyon and traveled as far north as what is today called Kansas.

7. Juan Rodríguez Cabrillo was responsible for exploring the Pacific coast in 1542. He was a Portuguese explorer that Spain hired. He and his men were probably the first Europeans to see what is now the California coast. They reached San Diego Bay. Part of the expedition, led by Bartolomé Ferrelo, sailed as far north as Oregon.

8. These explorers for Spain learned a lot about North America, but they found very little gold. Meanwhile, other Spanish explorers were finding great riches in Central and South America.

▲ Ponce de León wrote his autograph signature, above. On a separate sheet of paper try writing your name in such a fancy style.

Understanding What You Have Read

Write the name of the person from this list next to the statement that each might have made. Not all choices will be used.

Coronado   Piñeda   Cabrillo
de Soto   Estevanico   Ponce de León

_____ 1. I searched for the "Seven Cities of Gold" in the Southwest. Some of the men on my expedition reached the Grand Canyon.

_____ 2. I mapped the coast of the Gulf of Mexico.

_____ 3. I was a slave who survived the Narváez expedition and later guided Father Marcos de Niza into what is now Arizona and New Mexico.

_____ 4. I led a voyage northward along the coast of California.

_____ 5. I reached Florida and claimed it for Spain.

Building Geography Skills

Study the map. Then answer the questions.

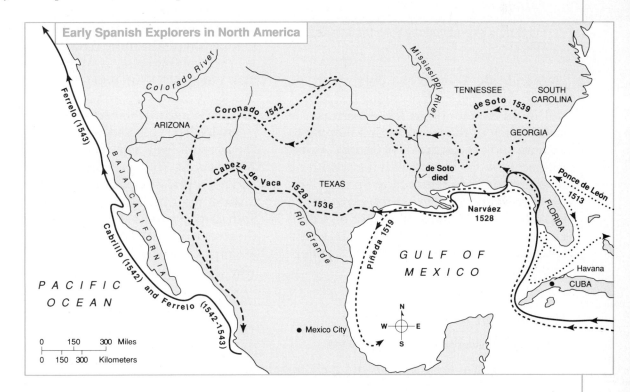

Early Spanish Explorers in North America

1. Who was the first explorer to see the east coast of Florida? _____

2. Who was the first explorer to cross what is now Georgia? _____

3. Who was the explorer to sail northward along the California coast to Oregon during 1543? _____

4. Who was the first explorer to cross what is now Texas? _____

▲ De Soto's expedition reaches the Mississippi River.

Hernando de Soto. When only about 14, Hernando de Soto left his home in Spain to sail in an expedition to the Americas. He spent much of the next 20 years helping to explore and conquer parts of Central America and Peru for Spain. With the wealth he obtained, de Soto returned to Spain. There he married and lived in luxury. However, in 1538, he was appointed governor of Cuba. He and his wife, Isabel de Bobadilla, sailed to Cuba, where de Soto organized a large expedition to Florida.

In 1539, de Soto appointed Isabel to act as governor of Cuba while he was away. Several hundred Spanish explorers led by de Soto sailed to the west coast of Florida. They landed near Tampa Bay. They were searching for riches, gold, silver, and jewels. At Tampa Bay they met Juan Ortiz, who had been part of the Narváez expedition. Ortiz had been captured by Native Americans and knew their language. In his 11 years living with Native Americans, he had heard stories of a rich land north of Tampa.

With Ortiz to interpret for them, de Soto and his group headed north. Near present-day Tallahassee, they captured, killed, and enslaved Native Americans who had attacked them. Then they moved into Georgia, where they met Cofita, a young Native American leader. She gave de Soto food, pearls, and furs. De Soto's group marched north into North Carolina and over the Smoky Mountains into Tennessee.

They continued on to Alabama, but their luck changed. Near what is now Mobile, they were ambushed and lost their supplies, the pearls, and all their religious equipment.

By 1541, de Soto and his men had reached the Mississippi River. They crossed it into Arkansas. De Soto was disappointed that he had not found any treasure. He turned back toward the Mississippi River. In 1542, de Soto died of a fever. His men buried him in the river to keep the Native Americans from learning of his death. Then they made their way to Mexico.

Recalling the Facts

Write your answer in the space provided.

1. What parts of the Americas did de Soto help explore and conquer before being appointed governor of Cuba? _____

2. Whom did de Soto appoint to govern Cuba when he was away? _____

3. What were the explorers on de Soto's expedition searching for in Florida? _____

   _____

4. List at least four states de Soto's expedition reached during its travels. _____

   _____

Using Primary Sources

Alvar Núñez Cabeza de Vaca was one of the survivors of the 1527 Narváez expedition. The survivors managed to reach the coast of Texas and spent several years wandering across western Texas and northern Mexico. They finally reached safety in Mexico. When Cabeza de Vaca returned to Spain, he wrote a book, *La Relación*, telling of the new land he had seen and his adventures there. It was one of the first written descriptions of the American Southwest and Florida.

> Here people have seen cattle. I have seen them three times and eaten them, and they seem to me to be the size of those in Spain. They have small horns like Moorish cattle, and the hair is very long and thick and curly, like a rug. Some are brown, others black, and they seem to me to have better and thicker meat than those in Spain. The Indians make blankets to cover themselves out of those that are not large, and from the largest, they make cloaks. One finds the animals for more than 400 leagues [about 350 miles] through all the land, and all along the way in the valleys. . . .
>
> Through these valleys in which we were, each one [explorer] carried a club the size of three handspans and everywhere rabbits went flying and jumping (so that we were stuffed with food). . . .
>
> Throughout the land [in Florida] we found a very great number of mosquitoes of three kinds. They were very nasty and annoying, and all the rest of the summer, they made us very tired. And to defend ourselves from them, we made many fires.

1. What do you think were the animals Alvar Núñez Cabeza de Vaca called "cattle"?

   _____

2. If you had been on this expedition, what would you have liked most? least?

   _____

   _____

CHAPTER REVIEW: CRITICAL THINKING

Classifying information means gathering facts and putting them into **categories**. Use the information in this chapter to classify the facts into three categories.

Explorer	Region Explored	Accomplishment
1. Ponce de León		
2.	Coast of the Gulf of Mexico	First European to reach the Mississippi River
3. Estevanico		
4.	California	Reached San Diego Bay
5. de Soto		Explored much of what is now a large section of the United States

Chapter 3

THE CONQUEST OF MEXICO AND PERU

AIMS: Who conquered Mexico? Who conquered Peru? Why were so few people able to conquer entire empires?

1. While some Spanish explorers were reaching new lands in La Florida, California, and elsewhere, others were conquering the Aztecs, the Mayans, and the Incas farther south. Two great empires had existed in Mexico—the Mayas and the Aztecs. For hundreds of years, the Mayas lived in the southern part of Mexico and in what is now Guatemala, Honduras, and Belize. The Mayas built many beautiful cities such as Tikal, which had about 40,000 people. They built great stone palaces and step-shaped pyramids. Women as well as men ruled the Mayan cities. Mayan experts developed a calendar. They wrote their history by carving picture symbols in stone.

2. During the late 800s, the Mayan empire began to weaken. Mayan city fought Mayan city. Rulers of conquered cities were killed and sacrificed to the Mayan gods. By the time the Spanish arrived, there were Mayan people, but no empire with a strong leader. Pedro de Alvarado led Spanish troops into Mayan lands in 1523. Spanish troops, led by Francisco de Montejo, conquered other parts of Mayan lands in the 1540s.

3. To the north of the Mayan lands, the Aztecs ruled the central part of Mexico. The Aztecs built their capital city of Tenochtitlán

▲ Spanish troops used guns and crossbows. What weapons did the Aztec troops use?

(tay-noch-tee-TLAN) on an island in Lake Texcoco. They turned swamps and islands into farming land. Early in the 1400s, they became the most powerful people in Mexico. Their weapons included spears, bows and arrows, and wood swords with sharp stone edges. The Aztecs were feared and hated by those whom they conquered. They would take gold, turquoise (a semiprecious stone), corn, animals, and slaves. Prisoners of war were sacrificed to Aztec gods.

4. In 1519, Hernando Cortés landed on the coast of Mexico. He was an explorer and conqueror. He wanted to take Mexico. He brought with him 700 Spanish soldiers, guns, and 18 horses. The Aztecs had never seen horses or guns before.

5. It did not take long for Cortés to conquer the Aztec empire. When the Aztec emperor, Moctezuma, heard about Cortés's arrival, he invited Cortés to his palace. Because of a legend, the Aztecs thought that Cortés might be the god Quetzalcoatl. That belief probably protected Cortés and his soldiers from being attacked by the Aztecs. Within a year, Cortés had gained control of Moctezuma and the Aztec empire. The Aztecs' enemies helped Cortés.

6. In 1520, Cortés left Pedro de Alvarado in charge of Tenochtitlán. He was cruel to the Aztecs. The Aztec citizens rose up in revolt against Alvarado. When Moctezuma tried to restore peace, the Aztecs killed him. Then they made Moctezuma's nephew, Cuauhtemoc, the new emperor. When Cortés returned to Tenochtitlán, the fighting continued. By the time Cortés had put down the revolt, Tenochtitlán was in ruins.

7. Thousands of miles to the south, another Spanish conqueror, Francisco Pizarro, was claiming the Inca empire. It was located in the Andes Mountains of Peru. Pizarro kidnapped and later killed the Inca emperor, Atahualpa. By the 1540s, the Spanish empire had control over the Inca empire, as well as the Aztec and Mayan empires.

Choose each correct answer and write the letter in the space provided.

_____ 1. The capital city of the Aztec empire was
    a. Tikal.
    b. Tenochtitlán.
    c. Cuzco.

_____ 2. The main idea of *paragraph 3* is that the Aztecs
    a. were miners of gold.
    b. had great power in central Mexico.
    c. feared a Spanish attack.

_____ 3. The Aztec emperor whom Cortés captured was
    a. Atahualpa.
    b. Moctezuma.
    c. Peruvian.

_____ 4. The conqueror of the Incas was
    a. Francisco Pizarro.
    b. Pedro de Alvarado.
    c. Francisco de Montejo.

_____ 5. The Aztecs built their capital city
    a. on an island in a lake.
    b. along the coast of the Gulf of Mexico.
    c. high in the Andes Mountains.

_____ 6. By the time the Spanish reached southern Mexico, the Mayas
    a. were at the peak of their power.
    b. welcomed them as allies against the Incas.
    c. no longer had an empire with a strong leader.

Building Geography Skills

Study the map. Then answer the questions.

1. Is South America southwest, southeast, or north of North America?

_____

2. Which early American empire was closest to the equator?

_____

3. Which early American empire was located farthest north?

_____

4. Which early American empire was located on the west coast of South America?

_____

5. List the early American empires shown in order of their land areas.

(a) the largest _____;

(b) second largest _____;

(c) smallest _____.

Early American Empires

NORTH AMERICA

GULF OF MEXICO

Tenochtitlán

ATLANTIC OCEAN

— 20°N

Tikal

20°N —

Aztecs

Veracruz

Mayas

Equator

SOUTH AMERICA

Machu Picchu

Cuzco

— 20°S

Incas

20°S —

PACIFIC OCEAN

— 40°S

40°S —

N
W—E
S

0   500   1000 Miles

0   500 1000 Kilometers

Spotlight on People

▲ Malinche translates as Cortés speaks with Moctezuma.

"Malinche," Doña Marina. Doña Marina was the name the Spanish *conquistadores* gave the young Native American woman who acted as their guide and translator. The Native Americans called her Malinche.

Malinche was born a princess. She was the daughter of a chief whose kingdom had been conquered by the Aztecs. She was going to inherit her father's titles when he died. When her father died, Malinche's mother remarried. The mother had a son and gave Malinche away to Native American traders so that her son could inherit the titles.

When Malinche was in her teens, she was sold to other Native American traders who gave her to Hernando Cortés. The conquistador discovered that she knew many Native American languages. That made her valuable, and she became Cortés's interpreter.

Malinche was also helpful in dealing with problems between the Spanish and the Native Americans. She became an adviser as well as a translator. At least once she saved Cortés and his men from danger.

Malinche had a son by Cortés. Later she married a member of the expedition. The couple went to Spain, where she died.

People today have different opinions about Malinche. Some think that she was a traitor for helping Cortés fight the Aztecs. Others say she got her revenge on the Aztecs for their cruelty to the people of her own conquered kingdom. Still others believe she herself had been badly treated by her own people. When the Spanish treated her well, she helped them. Still others say Malinche helped the Spanish because of her love for Cortés.

Recalling the Facts

Choose each correct answer and write the letter in the space provided.

_____ 1. Doña Marina was born
   a. a princess.
   b. a Spanish princess.
   c. to a Native American mother and a Spanish father.

_____ 2. Malinche lived
   a. all her life in Mexico.
   b. all her life in Spain.
   c. in Spain for a time.

_____ 3. Once doña Marina
   a. tried to kill Cortés.
   b. warned Cortés of danger.
   c. spied on the Spanish for her mother.

_____ 4. Malinche was valuable to the Spanish because she
   a. was close to her brother who was an Aztec chief.
   b. spoke several languages.
   c. had been trained as a spy.

_____ 5. Opinions today about Malinche
   a. are that she was a military genius.
   b. always blame her for helping Cortés.
   c. do not always agree.

Using Primary Sources

Bernal Díaz del Castillo was with Cortés when the Spanish entered Tenochtitlán. He wrote the history of that conquest. This is his description of the first Spanish view of the Aztec capital. Read the description. Then write the answers to the questions that follow.

> We saw so many cities and villages built in the water, and other great towns on dry land, and that straight and level causeway [raised road] going toward Mexico [Tenochtitlán]. We were amazed and said that it was like the enchantments they tell of in the legends . . . on account of the great towers . . . and buildings rising from the water, and all built of masonry [stone]. And some of our soldiers even asked whether the things we saw were not a dream. It is not to be wondered at that I here write it down in this manner, for there is so much to think over that I do not know how to describe it, seeing things that we did that had never been heard of or seen before, not even dreamed about.

1. What were some of the details that amazed the Spanish? _____

    _____

2. What were the buildings made of? Why do you think that amazed the Spanish?

    _____

CHAPTER REVIEW: CRITICAL THINKING

A **conclusion** is a reasonable guess about something. It is based on what you know or can reason out. Read the paragraphs below. Put a check next to the best conclusion. Then write a sentence to explain your choice.

1. The Aztecs spent much of their time following religious practices. Like Europeans, they went to war often. An important reason that the Aztecs fought so often was to take prisoners. The Aztecs used these prisoners as human sacrifices in religious ceremonies.

    _____ **a.** The Aztecs believed that the prisoners became gods.

    _____ **b.** The Aztecs thought that war was a religious duty.

    _____ **c.** War kept the Aztecs from their religious practices.

    Explain: _____

2. The Mayas developed an advanced civilization that lasted for hundreds of years. Stone monuments that still stand today record important dates and events in the lives of their rulers. Mayan books made from the bark of fig trees have also been found. These include calendars and information about religious ceremonies.

    _____ **a.** The Mayas had a system of writing.

    _____ **b.** The Mayas did not know how to read.

    _____ **c.** All Mayan records were about religion.

    Explain: _____

Chapter 4

THE SPANISH COLONIES

AIMS: How did Spain organize its colonies? What effects did Spanish rule have on Native Americans?

1. By 1600, Spain's colonies stretched from what is now the United States to the southern tip of South America. The Spanish king gave large areas of land to the *conquistadores* and to noble families. The people given the land were called **encomenderos**. The land was called an **encomienda**. It included the Native Americans who lived on the land. These people were forced to pay taxes or to work for their masters at low wages. In return, the landowners were supposed to protect the Native Americans and pay for a priest for them.

2. At first, Spanish settlers in some places had treated the Native Americans as slaves. New laws were passed to put an end to the slavery of Native Americans. Many *encomenderos* did not obey the new laws. Bartolomé de las Casas, a missionary and *encomendero*, told the king about the continued slavery and harsh treatment. Slavery was stopped on orders from Spain. However, Native Americans often remained poor and overworked by their masters. In the coastland and on the Caribbean islands, smallpox and other European diseases as well as harsh treatment wiped out entire communities. Spanish colonists along the coasts began to import slaves from Africa.

3. For Spain, mining was the most important economic activity in the Americas. The world's richest silver mines were in Mexico and Bolivia. Silver quickly replaced gold as the most important export shipped from the colonies to Spain. The Spanish treasure fleet was the envy of Europe.

4. Native Americans raised the landowners' crops. Some crops were new to the Americas. Colonists brought oranges, lemons, apples, pears, sugarcane, wheat, rice, and flax. Native Americans taught the colonists to grow products unknown to Europeans. These included potatoes, corn, yams, peanuts, tomatoes, pumpkins, and tobacco. The Spanish brought horses and mules to be used as work animals.

5. The Roman Catholic church's missionaries had been sent to the Americas along with the *conquistadores*. The Church set up **missions**. These were communities run by the Church. Their main purpose was to teach Christianity to the Native Americans.

6. In the growing Spanish towns, a small Spanish colonial group controlled the government and society. A few families ran the businesses. The Spanish built great cities. Mexico City was founded on the ruins of Tenochtitlán in 1521. The city had paved streets, a public water system, and a police force. Beautiful churches were built in the Spanish style. By 1551, the first universities had been set up in Mexico City and in Lima, Peru.

7. For a long time, there were few Spanish women in the colonies. Many Spanish families did not allow their unmarried daughters to go abroad. Thus, many colonists took Native American or black women as their wives. Today the languages, religions, music, and customs still reflect the mixture of people who settled the land.

▲ Native Americans were forced to work in these Bolivian silvermines. The nearby city of Potosí grew larger than any city in Spain.

Understanding What You Have Read

Choose each correct answer and write the letter in the space provided.

_____ 1. The right to use the land and the Native Americans who farmed it was called
    a. the *encomienda* system.
    b. slavery.
    c. the mission system.

_____ 2. The main idea in *paragraph 3* is that the most important product shipped back to Spain was
    a. sugar.
    b. silver.
    c. gold.

_____ 3. One of the first universities in the Americas was started in
    a. California.
    b. Mexico City.
    c. Florida.

_____ 4. For a long time there were few Spanish women in the colonies because many Spanish families
    a. did not allow their unmarried daughters to go outside Spain.
    b. were waiting for the *encomienda* system to end.
    c. sent their daughters to other parts of Europe instead.

_____ 5. Native Americans taught the Spanish about
    a. apples, pears, and wheat.
    b. oranges, lemons, and sugarcane.
    c. corn, tomatoes, and potatoes.

_____ 6. The Spanish brought to the Americas
    a. pumpkins and tobacco.
    b. horses and donkeys.
    c. peanuts and yams.

Daily Life

The Mission System. The Spanish set up missions which were a combination of school, church, farm, and work place. Pedro Menéndez de Avilés set up the first mission in what is now the United States. He founded it in 1565 in St. Augustine, on the east coast of Florida.

At the missions, the priests taught the Roman Catholic religion, the Spanish language, trades, farming, and Spanish ideas about government. The **missionaries** learned the Native American languages and made dictionaries. Children and adults were taught to read and write. The mission provided Native Americans who lived at the mission with food, clothing, and a place to live. In return, the Native Americans worked for the mission. Many became farmers or ranchers. Others made cloth, candles, metal objects, or furniture. Some missions raised animals.

Each day began with religious services. Then the grown-ups went to work and the children to school. After lunch, there was more work and more school.

Some Native Americans got used to the missions. Others learned enough to begin their own businesses. Many Native Americans, however, did not want to be forced to live at the mission. They wanted to return to their own ways of life. However, over the years, thousands of Native Americans were converted to Christianity. The Roman Catholic religion has been a powerful force in shaping the way millions of people in the Americas live today.

Complete each of the following sentences.

1. The first mission in what is now the United States was in _____.

2. The priests taught the Native Americans the _____ language.

3. The day began with _____.

4. A main goal of the missions was to convert the Native Americans to _____.

Bartolomé de las Casas. In 1502, Bartolomé de las Casas made his first voyage to the Americas. Later, he became the first Roman Catholic priest to be ordained in the New World. He was both a priest and an *encomendero*.

At first he did not think the use of Native Americans as forced laborers was wrong. Then, in 1515, he read a verse from the Bible that made him change his mind. The verse said, "He that sacrificeth of things wrongfully gotten, his offering is ridiculous, and the gifts of unjust men are not accepted." Las Casas began to speak out against the slavery of Native Americans and how it was killing them. Las Casas believed the *encomienda* system was not making them into Christians. It was only helping the Spanish become rich.

Las Casas said that enslaving Native Americans was a sin and the Spanish should set them free. In addition, he believed that the Spanish should give back all the gold, silver, jewels, and land that they had taken .

King Charles V gave Las Casas permission to settle land with Native Americans who would learn Christianity and be paid for their work. Then, in 1544, Las Casas became bishop of Chiapas in Mexico. The Spanish colonists united against Las Casas and forced him to flee into Nicaragua, where he continued his fight. The colonists did not want anyone telling them how to treat Native Americans.

Las Casas continued to fight for Native American rights. He wrote several books including *History of the Indies*. In 1547, Las Casas returned to Spain. He gave up being a bishop. In his *Very Brief Account of the Destruction of the Indies*, he wrote about the terrible treatment of the Native Americans. Because of his work to protect the Native Americans, who were called Indians, Las Casas is known as "the Apostle of the Indians."

Recalling the Facts

Choose each correct answer and write the letter in the space provided.

_____ **1.** Bartolomé de las Casas was the first
   a. *encomendero.*
   b. Dominican in the New World.
   c. Roman Catholic priest ordained in the New World.

_____ **2.** Las Casas's mind was changed when
   a. he read a verse in the Bible.
   b. settlers urged him to convert Native Americans.
   c. the king ordered him to return to Spain.

_____ **3.** After Las Casas became bishop of Chiapas,
   a. the settlers began to listen to his demands.
   b. the Native Americans rebelled.
   c. the colonists forced him to leave.

_____ **4.** Las Casas wrote books about
   a. the Dominican order.
   b. the history of the Indies.
   c. Mexico

The Arts and Technology

▲ This is the Taos Pueblo in New Mexico.

Pueblos. Many Native Americans in what is now New Mexico and Arizona lived in buildings that were homes for many families. Some of those apartment buildings were very big. One of the largest had over 800 rooms. The Spanish called these dwellings *pueblos,* the Spanish word for villages. They called the people who lived there Pueblo Indians.

The Pueblo Indians were actually members of several different tribes, language families, and groups. The main thing that they had in common was their many-storied dwellings. People had lived in some of these *pueblos* for more than 2,000 years.

1. Why did the Spanish think of these places as villages? _____

_____

_____

2. How is a *pueblo* different from other Native American homes you have read about?

_____

_____

CHAPTER REVIEW: CRITICAL THINKING ▉

You can **summarize** information, or write about it in a short way, to help you remember it. Reread *paragraphs 2, 3,* and *7.* Then write a one-line headline about what you have read.

Paragraph 2: _____

Paragraph 3: _____

Paragraph 7: _____

UNIT 1 REVIEW

Summary of the Unit

A few of the important events and facts presented in Unit 1 are listed below. On a separate sheet of paper, write these four and then add four more.

1. Columbus's first voyage began an age of Spanish exploration and discovery in the New World.
2. During the 16th century, Spanish explorers and *conquistadores* visited and mapped the east and west coasts of North America as well as large parts of the South and Southwest.
3. South of what is now the United States, Cortés conquered Mexico, and Pizarro conquered Peru.
4. Most colonists were interested in gold, silver, or free Native American labor. The Spanish government and Roman Catholic church wanted to convert the Native Americans to Christianity.

Understanding What You Have Read

Choose each correct answer and write the letter in the space provided.

_____ 1. The first 1,500 Spanish settlers in the New World came with
   a. Ponce de León.
   b. Amerigo Vespucci.
   c. Columbus on his second voyage.

_____ 2. One reason Cabeza de Vaca is important is that he
   a. was the first European to set foot on the mainland of what is now the United States.
   b. wrote a book describing what he saw in the New World.
   c. translated Native American books.

_____ 3. Cortés and Pizarro came looking for
   a. gold and silver.
   b. lost Spanish explorers.
   c. the Mayan empire.

_____ 4. The first woman to act as governor of a Spanish colony in the Americas was
   a. Malinche.
   b. Isabella of Castile.
   c. Isabel de Bobadilla.

_____ 5. The *encomienda* system for the most part
   a. resulted in good treatment for the Native Americans.
   b. treated Native Americans cruelly.
   c. did not help Spanish colonists.

_____ 6. One way many Native Americans died was
   a. from European diseases.
   b. in farm accidents.
   c. by sailing to Spain.

Building Your Vocabulary

Write the correct word next to the phrase that describes it. Not all choices will be used.

caravel	*conquistador*	*encomendero*	*encomienda*	admiral
mission	*voyage*	flax	*pueblo*	missionary

_____ 1. Spanish conqueror of Native Americans

_____ 2. a long trip by a water route

_____ 3. kind of sailing ship

_____ 4. person who came to convert Native Americans to Christianity

_____ 5. Spanish settler who received land and for whom Native Americans were forced to work

_____ 6. religious center that was a farm, school, and church combined

_____ 7. a Native American village built like an apartment building

_____ 8. system of forcing Native Americans to work for Spanish settlers

Developing Ideas and Skills—Time Lines

A time line helps us understand history. It shows us at a glance the order in which things happen. This time line shows events in the history of some early American empires. Study the time line. Then write your answers in the space following each question.

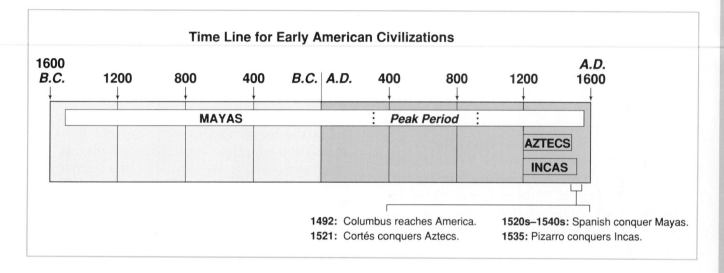

Time Line for Early American Civilizations

1. What was the earliest empire in the Americas?_____

2. Who came first, the Mayas or the Aztecs? _____

3. About how many years did the Inca empire last? _____

4. Did the peak of the Mayan empire happen before or after the arrival of the Spanish? _____

_____

Making History Live

1. Use a map of the United States to find Spanish place names. These can be names of such places as towns, rivers, states, and so forth. List at least ten places in different parts of the country that have Spanish names.

2. Choose one Spanish explorer or conqueror. Pick an important event in that person's life. Write a short report on that event, or draw a picture illustrating it.

3. Throughout history, people in one area have borrowed ideas, objects, and ways of doing things from people in other places. Here is a list of things people have borrowed from one part of the world or another. Make a list of them. For each item, make a guess and write whether you think the item was first used in *the Americas* or in *Europe*. Then use encyclopedias and other library reference books to find out how many of your answers are correct.

turkeys	sweet potatoes	rubber balls	canoes
white potatoes	corn	tomatoes	quinine medicine
cattle	chocolate	pigs	lima beans

Chapter 5 SETTLEMENT OF LA FLORIDA

AIMS: What area did La Florida include? Why and when did the Spanish begin to send settlers there?

1. At first, there was little interest in La Florida. The land did not have gold. La Florida was important mostly because of its location between the Caribbean islands and the Southwest. The Spanish treasure fleets could be protected by ships based in La Florida.

2. In 1526, Lucas Vázquez de Ayllón tried to settle La Florida. He received permission from Charles V, ruler of Spain, to explore the coast of La Florida. The king also made Ayllón **adelantado,** or governor. Ayllón set out from Hispaniola with 5 ships, 89 horses, and about 600 people. The people included 3 Dominican missionaries and African slaves. Women were also among these first settlers. Winds blew them farther north than they had planned. Ayllón and his group landed in what is now South Carolina. The Spanish named their colony San Miguel de Gualdape.

3. First they built a storehouse for their supplies and then homes and a place of worship. The cold winter was very hard for them. Many settlers became too sick to fish. Fish were a main source of food. Over 400 people died

▲ An artist's picture of St. Augustine about 100 years after the city was founded. Who was the person who founded this first permanent settlement in La Florida?

from disease and hunger. Ayllón died of malaria. Early in 1527, the remaining 150 colonists returned to Hispaniola. Although San Miguel de Gualdape was not permanent, it was the first European settlement in what is now the United States.

4. In 1559, Tristán de Luna y Arellano, governor of La Florida, tried to settle the land. He brought 500 soldiers, 1,000 colonists and their servants, and 240 horses to Ochuse. That is near present-day Pensacola, Florida. The colonists brought tools, food, and cattle and began to build a town. When a fierce storm struck the harbor, it destroyed several ships and all the supplies. Most of the people survived and found food. Later, de Luna decided to move the camp inland. He sent soldiers to find food because so many colonists were starving. De Luna also tried to set up a colony at Santa Elena, in present-day South Carolina. In 1560, the soldiers were no longer willing to follow orders. They replaced him as governor. No permanent colonies remained.

5. The first permanent settlement began at St. Augustine in 1565. King Philip II of Spain was worried because French Protestants, called Huguenots, had begun to settle at Fort Caroline. That was near the present-day city of Jacksonville, Florida. The king ordered Pedro Menéndez de Avilés to build a permanent settlement in Florida and drive out the Huguenots. After attacking and killing the French, Avilés explored along the Atlantic coast. He built seven settlements.

6. After the French were driven out Spain had problems with the British. The British had become enemies of Spain. British ships tried to attack the Spanish treasure fleets. In 1586, Sir Francis Drake, a British pirate, destroyed part of St. Augustine. Slowly, the people rebuilt it. By the late 1600s, more than a thousand people lived in St. Augustine. There were also at least 38 missions for Native Americans built across La Florida. Except for the years from 1763 to 1783, the Spanish flag flew over much of Florida from 1565 to 1821.

Answer each question in the space provided.

1. Why was the location of La Florida important to Spain? _____
    _____

2. What settlement was the first Spanish attempt to set up a colony on the North American
    mainland? _____

3. Who started the first permanent European settlement in North America? _____

4. What was the title of a governor of Spanish territory? _____

5. Spain controlled Florida for about how many years? _____

Building Geography Skills

Study the map. Then answer the questions.

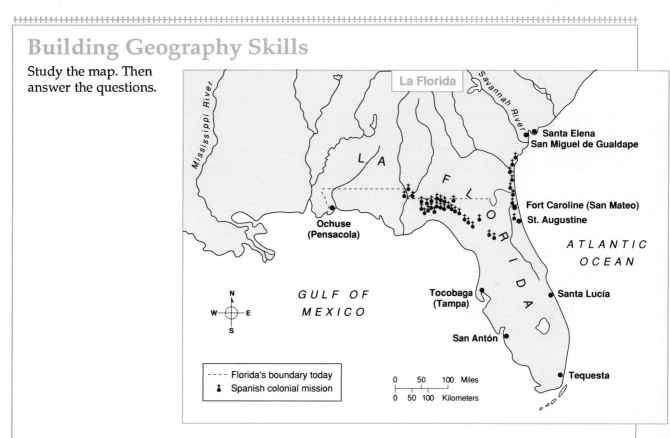

1. Was the area called La Florida larger or smaller than the state of Florida today?
    _____

2. Which early settlements were on the Atlantic coast of La Florida? _____
    _____

3. Which early settlements in La Florida were on the coast of the Gulf of Mexico? _____
    _____

4. Which settlements were northeast of where the Savannah River meets the ocean?
    _____

Pedro Menéndez de Avilés. Menéndez was born in Spain in 1519. He began sailing at an early age. Before he was 40, he was made captain general of the Indies fleet. The fleet was made up of treasure ships that brought gold, silver, and other riches from America to Spain. British, Dutch, and French ships had begun to attack some of the treasure ships. To keep the ships safe, Spain had to keep its Caribbean islands and La Florida.

The king asked Menéndez to establish a settlement and remove the French, who had settled on an important part of the Florida coast. In 1565, Menéndez arrived in St. Augustine Bay. He named the site St. Augustine since he first saw it on the Feast of St. Augustine. The Spanish began to build a fort there. Within a few weeks, Menéndez and his troops attacked the French Huguenots at Fort Caroline. The Spanish massacred most of the French.

Menéndez then set up a government at St. Augustine. It had military and civil officials and a hall of justice. He brought farmers, tradespeople, and women from Europe. The first European child, Martin Arguelles, was born in St. Augustine. Today St. Augustine is the oldest city in the United States.

Menéndez renamed Fort Caroline, calling it San Mateo. (It is now part of Jacksonville). In La Florida, he founded four other settlements. These were Santa Lucía, Tequesta (present-day Miami), San Antón, and Tocobaga (Tampa). Menéndez also founded Santa Elena in what is now South Carolina. He also set up missions. Shortly before his death, Menéndez wrote a letter from Spain to his nephew. He wrote, "After the salvation of my soul, there is nothing in this world I want more than to be in Florida, to end my days saving souls."

Recalling the Facts

Choose each correct answer and write the letter in the space provided.

_____ 1. The oldest *permanent* settlement in the United States is
a. San Miguel de Gualdape.
b. St. Augustine.
c. Jamestown.

_____ 2. King Philip II of Spain wanted Spanish settlers in La Florida because
a. he knew they would find gold.
b. they were needed as miners.
c. he wanted to protect the Spanish treasure ships.

_____ 3. The first thing Menéndez did was
a. build a fort.
b. shipwreck the French settlers.
c. set up a government.

_____ 4. Menéndez changed the name of Fort Caroline to
a. Santa Elena.
b. San Mateo.
c. Jacksonville.

_____ 5. Besides founding St. Augustine, Menéndez
a. set up other settlements and missions.
b. surrendered part of La Florida to the French.
c. searched for the Fountain of Youth in southern Florida.

The Arts and Technology

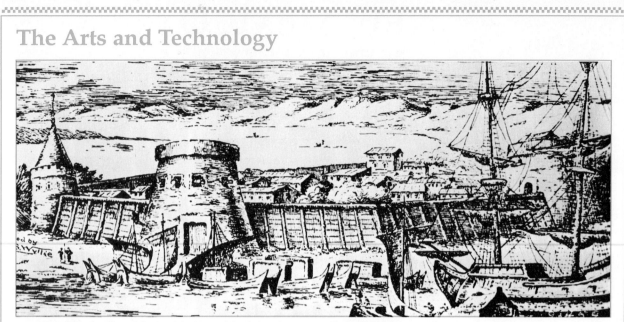

▲ Castillo de San Marcos is the oldest fort in the United States.

Castillo de San Marcos. All the early forts at St. Augustine were made of wood. They were difficult to defend. In 1671, Don Manuel de Cendaya was made governor of Florida. One of his orders was to build a stone fort at St. Augustine.

Spanish and Native American workers, convicts, and slaves began work in 1672. It took many years to complete the fort, which was named Castillo de San Marcos. Governor Laureano de Torres y Ayala, who was born in Havana, Cuba, completed the fort.

The Castillo de San Marcos had a V-shaped structure outside to protect the gate. It had a moat, a wide water-filled ditch, around the entire fort. Inside was a chapel and housing for soldiers. An arms storeroom and a storeroom for food and other goods were also there.

After Great Britain took over Florida in 1763, the fort was renamed Fort St. Mark. When Florida became part of the United States in 1821, the fort was renamed Fort Marion.

1. Why was a stone fort built? _____

_____

2. What kind of rooms did the Castillo de San Marcos have? _____

_____

CHAPTER SUMMARY: CRITICAL THINKING

When you read about almost any issue, you learn **different points of view**. Below are three statements about the events described in this chapter. They may have been made by the leader of Spain, England, or France. Write the words *Spain*, *England*, or *France* in the blank before each statement.

_____ 1. "Sir Francis Drake, attack the Spanish settlements in Florida."

_____ 2. "Set up forts on the coast to protect our treasure ships."

_____ 3. "It is an outrage that you massacred my subjects and changed the name of Fort Caroline."

Chapter 6 NEW MEXICO AND ARIZONA

AIMS: What Spanish leaders settled New Mexico and Arizona? How did the Native Americans respond to the Spanish?

1. More than 50 years after Coronado entered New Mexico in 1540, Juan de Oñate brought Spanish settlers north from New Spain. In 1598, Oñate, as governor of New Mexico, brought in soldiers, colonists, missionaries, and farm animals such as horses.

2. The Spanish settled at a place they called San Juan de Los Caballeros. The missionaries started working to convert the Pueblo Indians. Oñate began to explore the region for gold and for a water route to the Pacific. His explorations took him as far north as Kansas and southwest to the Gulf of California. When Oñate returned to New Mexico, his enemies accused him of treating the Pueblo Indians badly. In 1607, Oñate resigned.

3. Pedro de Peralta, a new governor, founded the city of Santa Fe in 1610. It was the third permanent city founded in what is now the United States (after St. Augustine in Florida and Jamestown in Virginia). Santa Fe is the oldest state capital in the United States.

4. Peralta built a government center at Santa Fe with Native American workers. He constructed the Palace of Governors. Peralta's government was run by citizens who owned property. They voted for members of their **cabildo,** or town council. Before long, prob-lems developed between government officials and church officials. Each accused the other of mistreating the Native Americans. These Native Americans had been doing most of the building, farming, and other work. They paid **tribute** to the Spanish. Tribute was a kind of tax, paid in corn, cloth, or work.

5. Native Americans were unhappy under the Spanish *encomienda* system. The first serious Native American rebellion came from the Apaches in 1676. Later, Popé, a Native American religious leader, united for a short time the different Native American peoples living in the *pueblos,* or villages. In 1680, Popé led these Pueblo Indians in an uprising. They wiped out most of the Spanish. Some of the Native Americans who had converted gave up Christianity. For a while, it seemed that Spanish settlement of New Mexico had ended. Even the horses, which the Spanish had forbidden Native Americans from owning, escaped. Twelve years passed before Diego de Vargas, a new governor, brought Spanish settlers back to New Mexico.

6. The settlement of Arizona took much longer for the Spanish. In the 1580s, silver had been found by the explorer Antonio de Espejo, but it was hard to reach and mine. Meanwhile, missionaries began to convert the Native Americans. In the 1690s, the Jesuit missionary Eusebio Kino set up missions in Arizona. He opposed the use of Native Americans as slaves in silver mines in Mexico.

◀ The Spanish explorer Oñate carved this message on a rock in New Mexico. It says, "Passed by here the Governor Juan de Oñate [on his way] to the discovery of the sea of the south in 16 April [in] year 1605."

A. Write the name of each person next to the statement that each might have made. Not all choices will be used.

| Pedro de Peralta | Popé | Eusebio Kino |
| Antonio de Espejo | Diego de Vargas | Juan de Oñate |

_____ 1. I found silver in Arizona.

_____ 2. I began the first Spanish settlement in what is now New Mexico.

_____ 3. I established Santa Fe as the capital of New Mexico.

_____ 4. I led the Pueblo Indians in an uprising against the Spanish.

_____ 5. I restored New Mexico to Spanish control.

B. In each of the sentences that follow, the underlined word or words make the sentence true or false. If the sentence is true, write **T** in the blank before it. If it is false, write the word or words that would make it true.

_____ 1. Spanish settlements in New Mexico began <u>a few years </u>after Coronado explored it.

_____ 2. Native Americans in New Mexico paid tribute in <u>gold</u> to the Spanish.

_____ 3. After the Pueblo uprising, it was <u>12</u> years before the Spanish recaptured New Mexico.

_____ 4. The town council was called a <u>*cabildo*</u>.

_____ 5. Santa Fe is the <u>oldest city </u>in the United States.

Building Geography Skills

Study the map. Then answer the questions.

1. Name two Spanish colonial towns in what is now Arizona._____

   _____

2. Name two Spanish colonial towns in what is now New Mexico._____

   _____

3. Wagon trains brought goods from Mexico City to the New Mexico missions. What was the name of the route used? _____

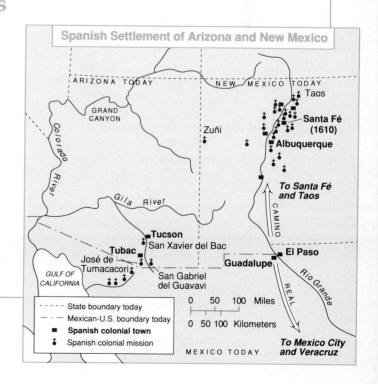

Spanish Settlement of Arizona and New Mexico

25 ▶

Diego de Vargas. Vargas was born in Spain. Both his parents came from wealthy, noble families. Vargas served at the Spanish court in Madrid before going to America.

Vargas was appointed governor of New Mexico in 1688. He did not take on the responsibility of that job until 1691. When he arrived in El Paso, a town then part of New Mexico, he was shocked to learn that his soldiers did not have enough equipment. There was also a shortage of supplies and food. The few remaining Spanish settlers were poor and starving. They wanted to leave New Mexico and move to Mexico. Vargas would not let the settlers leave. He began the reconquest of New Mexico.

Vargas left El Paso and captured the southern pueblos. He marched on to Santa Fe. With almost no fighting, Vargas was able to gain control of 77 pueblos. Then he returned to Mexico to gather new Spanish settlers.

By 1696, New Mexico was back under Spanish control. Vargas had ended Native American control and brought back Spanish settlers. The settlers and Native Americans would continue to have trouble. However, the area would never again come under Native American control.

Recalling the Facts

Choose each correct answer and write the letter in the space provided.

_____ 1. Diego de Vargas was born in
a. Mexico. b. Peru. c. Spain.

_____ 2. Vargas was upset to learn that
a. there was a shortage of food and supplies for his troops.
b. he could not travel with the wagon train.
c. Spanish settlers did not want to move to Mexico.

_____ 3. After Vargas took the southern pueblos, he
a. went back to Spain.
b. brought settlers to New Mexico.
c. sent soldiers back to Mexico.

_____ 4. In 1698, New Mexico
a. was controlled by Pueblo Indians.
b. had no Spanish settlers left.
c. was back in Spanish hands.

_____ 5. Vargas is important because he
a. built a capital at Santa Fe.
b. began Spanish difficulties with the Native Americans.
c. regained control of New Mexico for Spain.

_____ 6. Vargas held the job of
a. general of the Spanish army.
b. governor of Mexico.
c. governor of New Mexico.

The Arts and Technology

The Palace of the Governors in Santa Fe. The Palace of the Governors was built in 1610, when Pedro de Peralta was governor. It was the center of government in New Mexico and is the oldest government building in what is now the United States. It is also the center of the city of Santa Fe.

When he was made governor, Peralta was ordered to find a new capital for New Mexico. He was to move the settlers to the new capital and build churches and public buildings there.

The Palace of the Governors shows the influence of the method of building used by the Pueblo Indians. This method uses materials found in the area. The Palace of the Governors is built of **adobe**. Wooden poles and crossbeams support the building.

Like other Spanish colonial government buildings, this one looks out on an open area or public square called a **plaza**. A church is also on the plaza.

Today, the plaza in front of the Palace of the Governors is sometimes used as an open-air Native American market. The building itself is now a museum.

▲ The walls of the Palace of the Governors are built of adobe. **Adobe** is a bricklike building material made of sun-dried earth and straw. What is the open area or public square in front of the building called?

Select a government building in your community or in a nearby one. What purpose does it serve? Briefly compare it to the Palace of the Governors.

_____

_____

_____

CHAPTER REVIEW: CRITICAL THINKING

If your shoelace is untied, it may cause you to trip. If you trip, it is the effect, or result, of the untied shoelace. **Recognizing causes and effects** can help you understand history. Read each of the effects listed below. From the information in this chapter, decide what might have been the cause. Write the cause in the line before each effect.

1. **Cause:** _____

   Effect: Many Pueblo Indians joined in the uprising against the Spanish in 1680.

2. **Cause:** _____

   Effect: By the early 1700s, the Plains Indians were experts at using horses to hunt buffalo.

7 SETTLEMENT OF TEXAS

AIMS: Why did it take so long for the Spanish to settle in Texas? What events led to Spanish settlements there?

1. Although Piñeda, Núñez Cabeza de Vaca, and Coronado explored parts of Texas in the 1500s, Spain did not try to settle Texas until the 1680s. Why? One reason was that no gold was found in Texas. The Spanish rulers needed money for wars in Europe, and Texas had no known riches.

2. In 1682, the French explorer La Salle explored the Mississippi River. La Salle called the area through which the Mississippi flowed Louisiana. He claimed it for France. He also hoped to build a fort and to invade and conquer part of Mexico. In 1684, he landed at Matagorda Bay along the Texas coast of the Gulf of Mexico. There he built Fort St. Louis.

3. The Spanish did not want the French to have Texas. As early as 1682, Spanish missionaries had built missions near El Paso. The governor of New Spain (present-day Mexico) sent Captain Alonso de León to remove the French from Texas. In 1689, de León found the ruins of Fort St. Louis. The French had been massacred by Native Americans. In 1690, de León returned to east Texas with a missionary who set up the first mission in that region. It was called San Francisco de los Tejas. (The word *Tejas* came from the Native American word meaning "friends.") The mission was abandoned in 1693 after many Native Americans had died of European diseases.

4. The Marqués de San Miguel de Aguayo set up a new capital for the province of Tejas. (The word *marqués* is a Spanish title of nobility.) The new capital was Los Adaes, which was across the border in France's colony of Louisiana. On his way back from Los Adaes, Aguayo set up **presidios** (forts) and missions. The only presidio-mission that succeeded was San Antonio de Valero, built in 1718. This and the nearby fort became known as San Antonio de Bexar. Together they were the start of the modern city of San Antonio.

5. Some Spanish settlers had the title *hidalgo*, or gentleman. In Spain, *hidalgos* had a strict code of honor that did not allow work by hand, such as farming. The settlement had trouble growing enough food.

6. Missions in Texas were often attacked by Native Americans. There were not enough Spanish soldiers to protect the settlers. The Spanish king sent the Marqués de Rubí to find out how to protect Texas. Rubí said that the settlers should leave all the missions except those in San Antonio and one other. Rubí also said that the Spanish, with the help of other Native Americans, should make war on the Apaches. The Apaches were seen as Spain's greatest Native American enemy in Texas. The Comanches were also an enemy.

7. Some east Texas settlers had not wanted to move to San Antonio, where the best land had already been taken. Their leaders asked to return. They were allowed to move back to east Texas. Finally in 1821, Mexico gained independence from Spain. Texas was part of the newly independent nation of Mexico.

▲ Native Americans dig an irrigation ditch at a Spanish mission in Texas. What was the main purpose of such missions?

Write the best word or phrase to complete each sentence.

1. At first, the Spanish were not interested in Texas because it didn't have _____.

2. The Spanish started to settle in Texas because they were afraid that the _____ would try to settle there.

3. The word *Tejas* comes from a Native American word meaning _____.

4. The new capital of Los Adaes was actually in _____.

5. The most successful presidio-mission was near the modern city of _____.

6. The soldiers could not _____ the land.

7. The Marqués de Rubí said that the _____ Indians were Spain's greatest enemy.

8. In the year _____, Mexico gained it independence from Spain, and Texas was a part of that new nation.

Building Geography Skills

Study the map. Then answer the questions.

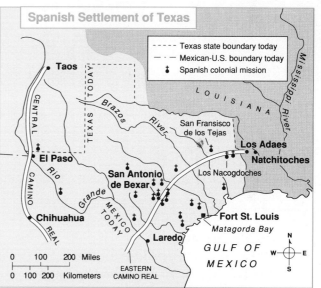

1. What was the name of the French-built fort on the coast of Texas at Matagorda Bay?

   _____

2. What two early Spanish settlements were in French-ruled Louisiana? _____

   _____

3. If you were traveling along the Eastern Camino Real from San Antonio de Bexar to Los Nacogdoches, in what general direction would you be going? _____

   _____

4. Were most Texas missions located in northern, eastern, or western Texas?

   _____

Spotlight on People

Antonio Gil Ybarbo. Antonio Gil Ybarbo was a member of a small Spanish group of settlers in east Texas. They moved onto the land in the piney woods without any help from the Spanish government. They farmed the land and raised the animals. They got along well with the Native Americans.

On the Marqués de Rubí's suggestion, the settlers in east Texas were ordered to move to San Antonio. Ybarbo and his neighbors did not want to leave their land. They considered San Antonio a more dangerous place, because the Apaches and Comanches often raided the San Antonio area. Yet they were forced to leave before they gathered the crops they had planted.

At San Antonio, they discovered that the missionaries, soldiers, and *hidalgos* had the best land.

Antonio Gil Ybarbo asked that the group be permitted to move back to their homes in the east. They were allowed to move but not as far east as their old homes. They moved to Bucareli in 1774, and for a while they were fine. Then in the spring and fall of 1778, Comanches stole their horses. Ybarbo and his friends asked for help from Spanish soldiers. The group was told there were not enough soldiers to send to help them.

In 1779, Antonio Gil Ybarbo's group decided to move all the way back to east Texas. They moved to where the presidio of Nacogdoches had been. Ybarbo built a stone fort and became lieutenant governor of Nacogdoches. The settlers remained there. Their descendants were still living there in the 20th century.

▲ Ybarbo and settlers reach the abandoned mission of Nacogdoches.

Recalling the Facts

Choose each correct answer and write the letter in the space provided.

_____ 1. When Ybarbo and his neighbors first settled in east Texas, the government
   a. set up a presidio for them.
   b. gave them Native Americans to farm the land.
   c. did not help them.

_____ 2. The land in east Texas was
   a. difficult to farm.
   b. a piney woods.
   c. often attacked by Native Americans.

_____ 3. Ybarbo and his neighbors moved to San Antonio because
   a. they thought there was better land in San Antonio.
   b. the government forced them.
   c. it was less dangerous there.

_____ 4. The best land in San Antonio was
   a. given to Ybarbo and his neighbors.
   b. already taken.
   c. farmed by Apaches and Comanches.

_____ 5. Ybarbo and his neighbors left Bucareli because
   a. the government forced them to leave.
   b. the land was not good for farming.
   c. Comanches stole their horses.

_____ 6. When Ybarbo and his neighbors left Bucareli, they moved to
   a. San Antonio.
   b. Nacogdoches.
   c. Louisiana.

The Arts and Technology

This is a copy of a hand-drawn map of San Antonio. The Marqués de San Miguel de Aguayo drew the map in the 1720s. As you have learned, San Antonio began with two settlements—the Mission San Antonio de Valero and the presidio San Antonio de Bexar. The Spanish began both settlements in 1718. Later, missions from eastern Texas moved to the San Antonio area. In the early 1730s, people from the Canary Islands (Spanish islands off the northwest coast of Africa) also settled in the area. Study the map. Then answer the questions.

1. What kinds of crops did the Native Americans grow?

   _____

   _____

2. How did farm areas get water?

   _____

   _____

   _____

3. What kinds of buildings are at each mission?

   _____

   _____

   _____

4. Why do you think the settlers built the *presidio* **where** they did? (**Hint:** What surrounds the land on which the

   presidio is built?) _____

   _____

   _____

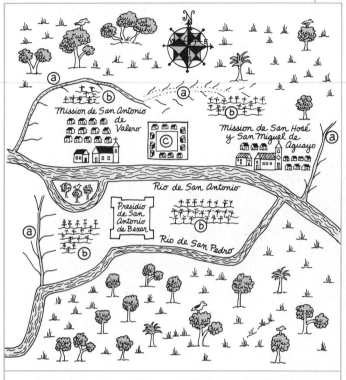

a. Acequia systems. These are ditches to bring water to the farm land.
b. Farm areas. Crops include maize (corn) and wheat.
c. Planned place for *hidalgos* to settle when they arrived in the 1730s.

CHAPTER REVIEW: CRITICAL THINKING

You can **summarize** information or write it in a few key sentences to help you remember it. Reread *paragraphs 1, 4,* and *5.* Then write a one- or two-line headline about what you have read in each of these paragraphs.

1. *Paragraph 1:* _____

   _____

2. *Paragraph 4:* _____

   _____

3. *Paragraph 5:* _____

   _____

Chapter 8 SETTLEMENT OF CALIFORNIA

AIMS: Why did the Spanish decide to begin settlements in California? How did they establish the settlements?

1. The name *California* was used for a large area. It included Baja (Lower) California, the peninsula that is now part of Mexico, and Upper California. The Spanish called the region California after the name of a treasure island from a Spanish novel. The Spanish had explored Upper California along the coast in the 1500s, but they had not settled there.

2. The Spanish decided to settle Upper California, because Spain was afraid that other nations might take the land. (As you have learned, this had been the case in Florida and Texas.) Spain noticed that the Russian fur trade was moving southward along the Pacific coast.

3. In 1769, Gaspar de Portolá, governor of Baja California, was ordered to begin settlements in Upper California. Father Junípero Serra, a Franciscan missionary, had the job of setting up the religious missions. Portolá set up the first presidio in 1769 at San Diego. Father Serra set up the first mission in Upper California in the same year.

4. The Spanish planned three kinds of settlements. These were the missions, the presidios, and the *pueblos*. You have already read about the missions and the presidios. The *pueblos* were towns where the rest of the Spanish colonists would live.

5. The Spanish had the missions built close to where the Native Americans lived. By the 1820s, they had built 21 missions in Upper California, each about a day's walk from the next. Missionaries and soldiers did not get along well. Each group accused the other of mistreating the Native Americans.

6. The mission land did not actually belong to the Church. The land was supposed to be held for Christian Native Americans. When the Spanish thought these Native Americans were ready to care for the land, it was to be given to them.

7. In 1821, Mexico won its independence from Spain. California was now part of Mexico. The Mexican government passed the Secularization Act in 1833. *Secularization* means changing something from religious control to civil, or nonreligious, control. Under the act, mission property was to be divided among the Native Americans and sold to settlers. Missions would become ordinary churches. Most Native Americans received land under the Secularization Act. However, most of them soon lost their land. They sold their land, were legally tricked out of it, or had it violently taken away. Most Native Americans ended up working for rich landowners at low wages.

8. The Mexican government made land grants of huge areas of land called **ranchos**. Even smaller ranchos had about 50,000 acres. By the 1840s, there were more than 800 ranchos in California. The owners, or **rancheros**, raised cattle for the hides, or skins, and for tallow. Tallow is fat used in making candles, soap, and other items. Most rancheros were Spanish or Mexican. People from the United States who married into ranchero families were also called rancheros. Rancheros had many servants. They also hired **vaqueros**, or cowboys, who looked after the cattle.

▲ Pictured are *Vaqueros* and sheepherders. What were the main products that California *ranchos* produced from their cattle?

In each of the sentences that follow, the underlined word or words make the sentence true or false. If the sentence is true, write **T** in the blank before it. If the sentence is false, write the word or words that would make it true.

_____ 1. One reason the Spanish wanted to settle California was that the <u>French</u> were moving southward along the coast.

_____ 2. Father Junípero Serra was a <u>Jesuit</u> missionary.

_____ 3. California settlements had missions, <u>presidios</u>, and pueblos.

_____ 4. The <u>Secularization Act</u> was supposed to take property out of the Church's control.

_____ 5. Most Native Americans received <u>large land grants</u>.

_____ 6. The rancheros raised cattle for their <u>meat</u>.

_____ 7. <u>Gaspar de Portolá</u> had the job of setting up Spanish forts in Upper California.

_____ 8. The Spanish chose places near where Native Americans lived to build their <u>universities</u>.

_____ 9. Mission land was supposed to be held in trust for <u>rancheros</u>.

_____ 10. In 1821, California became part of <u>the United States</u>.

Building Geography Skills

Study the map. Then answer the questions.

1. How many miles would a traveler go from Santa Barbara to Monterey if he or she stopped at four missions along the way?_____

_____

2. Name two presidios shown on the map._____

_____

_____

3. In 1812, the Russians built a fur-trading post at Fort Ross. Was the fort north, south, east, or west of San Francisco?

_____

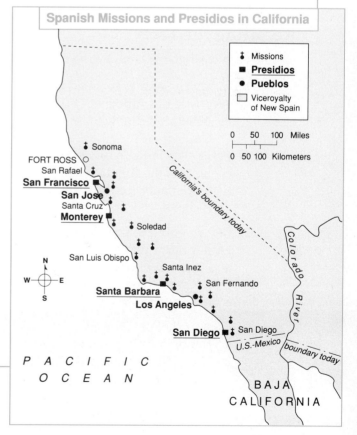

Spanish Missions and Presidios in California

Missions
Presidios
Pueblos
Viceroyalty of New Spain

0 50 100 Miles
0 50 100 Kilometers

Spotlight on People

Father Junípero Serra. Junípero Serra was sometimes called the "Apostle of California." An apostle is the first person in a place to teach the Christian religion.

Father Serra was born in Majorca, a Spanish island near Spain, in 1713. He became a priest and a Franciscan. He was a well-known speaker, thinker, and college teacher before he decided to go to Mexico in 1749. In Mexico, he worked as a missionary. Then he was sent to Baja California.

When Gaspar de Portolá was sent on a military mission to Upper California, Father Serra was asked to go along. He was in charge of a group of 17 missionaries.

The trip to Upper California was difficult for Father Serra because he was disabled in one leg. Yet he felt strongly that he was doing God's will in converting the Native Americans. In 1769, he set up the first mission, San Diego de Alcalá, in present-day San Diego. Before he died in 1784, Father Serra set up eight more missions. Others added more missions until there were 21 missions in all.

Father Serra is considered to be the person most responsible for starting Spanish settlements in California.

Recalling the Facts

Choose each correct answer and write the letter in the space provided.

_____ 1. Junípero Serra was called the "Apostle of California" because
  a. he explored new areas of California.
  b. he was lame in one leg.
  c. he was the first to teach Christianity to the California Indians.

_____ 2. Before going to California, Father Serra was
  a. a teacher and a missionary.
  b. a Jesuit priest.
  c. a Spanish soldier.

_____ 3. Gaspar de Portolá was
  a. the best young missionary.
  b. the military leader in California.
  c. in charge of 17 missionaries.

_____ 4. Father Serra set up a total of
  a. one mission.
  b. nine missions.
  c. twenty-one missions.

_____ 5. One reason that the trip to Upper California was difficult for Father Serra was that
  a. he did not believe in what he was doing.
  b. no Spanish explorers had ever been to California before.
  c. he was lame in one leg.

_____ 6. Father Serra is important because
  a. he began settlements in Upper California.
  b. he gave land to Native Americans.
  c. he directed the presidios.

The Arts and Technology

The Santa Barbara Mission. The mission at Santa Barbara was set up in 1786. The present building was built in 1815 and combines Spanish and Moorish architecture. The roof is made of clay tiles. The columns and walls with curved openings are called arches. The church has two large towers that contain bells. The mission was named for the patron saint of sailors.

▲ This is a hundred-year-old photo of the Santa Barbara mission.

1. What do you think the aqueduct, or water-filled canal, in the picture was used for?

   _____

   _____

2. What is the largest building in the mission used for? _____

   _____

   _____

3. Briefly compare this architecture with the architecture of a house of worship in your

   community. _____

   _____

   _____

CHAPTER REVIEW: CRITICAL THINKING

The Spanish government wanted to keep its colonies for Spanish settlers only. Spain did not permit people from other countries to stop at ports in California. The Spanish did not permit others to travel or settle in Spanish colonies.

1. Why did the policy of allowing only Spanish to settle in Spanish colonies make it difficult

   for the colonies to grow? _____

   _____

2. What might have happened if people from other countries had been allowed to settle in

   Spanish colonies? _____

   _____

UNIT 2 REVIEW

Summary of the Unit

A few of the important events and facts presented in Unit 2 are listed below. Write these in your notebook and add three more.

1. Spain set up colonies in La Florida, New Mexico, Arizona, Texas, and California when other countries became interested in the land.
2. In each colony, soldiers and missionaries began the settlement and tried to convert local Native Americans.
3. In the Spanish colonies, missionaries and soldiers disagreed about the treatment of the Native Americans.

Understanding What You Have Read

Choose each correct answer and write the letter in the space provided.

_____ 1. The first colony in what is now the United States was in
   a. La Florida.
   b. New Mexico.
   c. Texas.

_____ 2. The colony at St. Augustine was started by
   a. Lucas Vázquez Ayllón.
   b. Tristán de Luna y Arellano.
   c. Pedro Menéndez de Avilés.

_____ 3. The Pueblo Indians staged a successful uprising in
   a. Texas.
   b. Florida.
   c. New Mexico.

_____ 4. Father Eusebio Francisco Kino established missions in
   a. Florida.
   b. Spain.
   c. Arizona.

_____ 5. After the Secularization Act, most land in California belonged to
   a. Native Americans.
   b. missionaries and churches.
   c. rancheros.

_____ 6. Countries that caused the Spanish to worry about land claims were
   a. Germany, Peru, and Argentina.
   b. Russia, Britain, and France.
   c. Mexico, France, and Italy.

Building Your Vocabulary

Write the correct word next to the phrase that tells about it.

plaza   cabildo   adelantado   hidalgo   mission
presidio pueblo   rancho   tallow   vaquero

_____ 1. beef fat used in making candles and soap

_____ 2. Spanish word for town

_____ 3. a Spanish gentleman

_____ 4. military fort

_____ 5. large area of private land

_____ 6. cowboy

_____ 7. town council

_____ 8. center of activity for converting Native Americans

_____ 9. open area or public square

_____ 10. governor

A. This is a picture of San Miguel Chapel in Santa Fe. It is said to be the oldest church in the United States. Study the picture. Then answer the questions.

1. What is this church probably built of:

   adobe, cement, or wood? _____

2. In what ways is it similar to and different from the church shown on page 35?

   _____

   _____

   _____

   _____

3. Using the information you learned about the date Santa Fe was founded, which of the following dates is probably the date this church was built: 1527, 1636, 1952?

   _____

B. Study the time line. Then answer the questions by writing the letter for the correct period of time in the space provided.

1500	1550	1600	1650	1700	1750	1800	1850
A	B	C	D	E	F	G	

_____ **1.** Santa Fe was founded.

_____ **2.** Spain builds its first permanent settlements in La Florida.

_____ **3.** The first presidio in Upper California is established.

_____ **4.** Mexico gains independence from Spain.

Making History Live

1. Choose one place mentioned in this unit. Find out what it is like today. Use your school library and public library for additional information. Some places to choose from are St. Augustine, San Antonio, Santa Fe, San Diego.
2. Write a report on one group of Native Americans mentioned in this unit.
3. Make a map or clay model of an early settlement in Florida, New Mexico, Arizona, Texas, or California.

Chapter 9 SPAIN GAINS THEN LOSES LOUISIANA

AIMS: How did Spain gain Louisiana? What difficulties did Spain have in Louisiana? How did Spain lose Louisiana?

1. From 1756 to 1763, Great Britain and France fought the Seven Years' War. This war was known in America as the French and Indian War. In 1762, Spain joined the war on the side of France. France secretly gave Louisiana to Spain. However, Great Britain won the war. The 1763 Treaty of Paris officially ended the war and gave the following to Great Britain: Florida, which had been a Spanish colony, and Canada, which had been a French colony. Also France officially gave its Louisiana colony to Spain.

2. Spain planned to use its new colony of Louisiana to protect Texas and Mexico from the military forces in Great Britain's nearby colonies. The first Spanish governor of Louisiana did not arrive until 1766. He was Antonio de Ulloa, a naval officer, a well-known scientist, and a writer. Ulloa arrived with only 90 Spanish soldiers. Charles Philippe Aubry, the last French governor, agreed to help Ulloa.

3. The settlers hoped that Spain would solve Louisiana's trade problems. Louisiana had little gold or silver. The paper money had no real value. That made it hard to do business. Ulloa arrived with money to pay government bills, but afterward Spain was slow in sending money. Then Spain ordered Louisiana to trade mainly with Spanish colonies and to use Spanish ships. The merchants of Louisiana objected. Their regular markets were elsewhere. Meanwhile, Ulloa began to strengthen forts in Louisiana. He built forts along the Mississippi River, across from British forts. He also began collecting **duties**, or taxes, on goods.

4. The settlers were unhappy with the way Ulloa governed. In 1768, a few French officials led the settlers in a rebellion. They forced Ulloa to leave. They claimed the right to choose their own form of government. Aubry governed the colony until Spain sent troops and Alexander O'Reilly to end the rebellion.

5. After O'Reilly restored peace, other Spanish governors took over. Bernardo de Gálvez served during the American Revolution. Gálvez sided with the American colonists, though Spain was at first neutral. Gálvez welcomed settlers to Louisiana. He saw it as a way for the area to grow. He let American Tories, who sided with the British, move to Louisiana. The American Tories had to swear loyalty to the king of Spain. The next governor, Esteban Rodríguez Miró, even encouraged settlers to leave United States territory and settle in Louisiana. Meanwhile, American citizens to the east of the Mississippi resented Spanish control of the river at its mouth. In 1784 Miró closed the river to American trade.

6. In 1800, Napoleon Bonaparte, the new ruler of France, forced Spain secretly to give Louisiana back to France. Then, in 1803, Napoleon sold Louisiana to the United States. Spain had ruled Louisiana for almost 40 years.

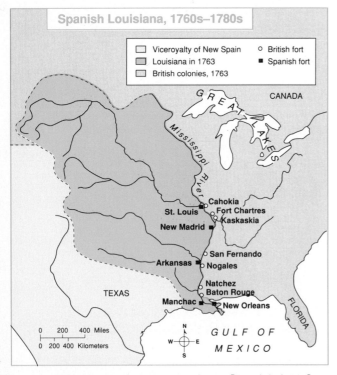

Spanish Louisiana, 1760s–1780s

☐ Viceroyalty of New Spain ○ British fort
▨ Louisiana in 1763 ■ Spanish fort
☐ British colonies, 1763

CANADA

GREAT LAKES

Mississippi River

Cahokia
St. Louis Fort Chartres
Kaskaskia
New Madrid

San Fernando
Arkansas Nogales
Natchez
Baton Rouge
Manchac New Orleans

TEXAS

FLORIDA

GULF OF MEXICO

0 200 400 Miles
0 200 400 Kilometers

N W E S

▲ What were the names of two Spanish forts?

Understanding What You Have Read

Write the names of the persons below next to the statement that each might have made.

Antonio de Ulloa   Charles Philippe Aubry   Alexander O'Reilly
Bernardo de Gálvez   Esteban Rodríguez Miró   Napoleon Bonaparte

_____ **1.** I was the first Spanish governor of Louisiana, but rebels forced me out.

_____ **2.** I won back Louisiana for Spain after the rebellion in 1768.

_____ **3.** I was the former French governor of Louisiana who worked with the Spanish governor.

_____ **4.** I encouraged American Tories to settle in Louisiana.

_____ **5.** I urged settlers from U. S. territory to come to Louisiana.

_____ **6.** I sold Louisiana to the United States in 1803.

|||||||||||||||||||||||||||||||||||||||||||||||||||||||||||||||||||||||||||||||||||||||||||||||||||||||||||

Linking Past to Present

Study the time line. Then answer the following questions.

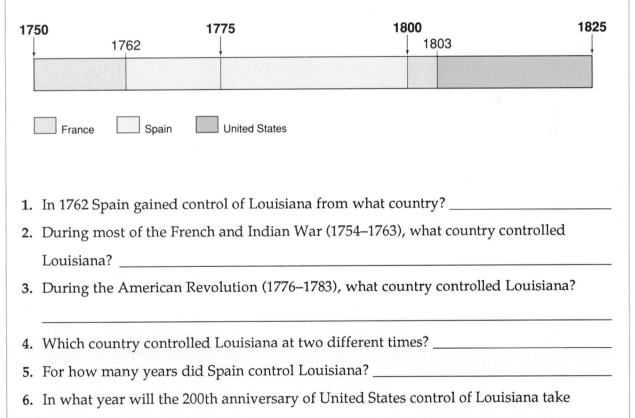

Control of Louisiana

1. In 1762 Spain gained control of Louisiana from what country? _____

2. During most of the French and Indian War (1754–1763), what country controlled Louisiana? _____

3. During the American Revolution (1776–1783), what country controlled Louisiana?

   _____

4. Which country controlled Louisiana at two different times? _____

5. For how many years did Spain control Louisiana? _____

6. In what year will the 200th anniversary of United States control of Louisiana take place? _____

Alexander O'Reilly. Spain's rule in Louisiana did not begin smoothly. After rebels forced Governor Antonio de Ulloa to leave Louisiana, Spain sent Alejandro (Alexander) O'Reilly to end the rebellion.

O'Reilly was born in Dublin, Ireland, in 1722. He joined the Spanish army and was promoted rapidly. In 1762, he was assigned to Cuba to organize the Cuban black militia.

Lieutenant General Alexander O'Reilly arrived in New Orleans in August 1769 with 24 ships and 2,600 soldiers. Just after arriving, he arrested 11 French leaders of the revolt. After a trial, five of them were executed by firing squad. Others were jailed.

O'Reilly reorganized the government of the colony. He declared Spanish the official language and said that Spanish laws were in force. Governor O'Reilly set up a *cabildo,* a council, to help him govern. He promoted trade and friendly relations with the Native Americans. When he left Louisiana in March 1770, the territory was at peace and on the road to prosperity.

After he returned to Spain, General O'Reilly received command of an army of 22,000 men for a campaign in North Africa. O'Reilly's army was defeated in 1775. King Charles III then assigned him to various positions in Spain. He died in 1794.

Recalling the Facts

Choose each correct answer and write the letter in the space provided.

_____ 1. O'Reilly was born in
   a. Cuba.
   b. Louisiana.
   c. Ireland.

_____ 2. Before his assignment in Louisiana, O'Reilly
   a. organized troops in Cuba.
   b. fought against Spain.
   c. led an army in North Africa.

_____ 3. O'Reilly punished the leaders of the rebellion by
   a. jailing them all.
   b. shooting them all.
   c. shooting some and jailing others.

_____ 4. Spanish became Louisiana's official language
   a. when Spain first gained Louisiana.
   b. under O'Reilly's rule.
   c. at no time during Spanish rule.

_____ 5. The purpose of the *cabildo* was to
   a. make new laws for Spain.
   b. help the Spanish govern.
   c. encourage trade.

_____ 6. After he left Louisiana, O'Reilly
   a. won new battles for Spain.
   b. had a brilliant military career.
   c. lost a war in Africa.

Using Primary Sources

Antonio de Ulloa did not have enough soldiers to govern Louisiana well. He and the former French governor had a joint French-Spanish rule. Although Ulloa raised the Spanish flag over Louisiana, he never performed the ceremony that made Louisiana officially Spanish.

Alexander O'Reilly took formal possession as soon as he arrived. Here is a description of that ceremony on August 18, 1769, written by O'Reilly's assistant, Lieutenant Colonel Francisco Bouligny. Read the description and then write the answers to the questions that follow.

> Everything was ready for the 18th when possession was taken of the plaza with all the form and ceremony appropriate. Our troops in the center of the plaza occupied three sides of a square and the French soldiers closed the square. The General disembarked [got off his ship] at 5:30 P.M. and came to the center of the plaza, where he presented to Monsieur Aubry . . . the order of His Catholic Majesty [Charles III of Spain]. Immediately [Aubry] placed at [O'Reilly's] feet the keys of the city. At the same time Spanish flags were run up in various parts of the city, and the artillery and the troops on the plaza fired a general salute. After this, our General, with the French commander and all the officers, whose duties permitted them, entered the church, where a Te Deum [hymn to God] was sung as an act of thanksgiving.

1. What official document did General O'Reilly show Aubry? _____

   _____

2. What act by the French governor showed he was handing over the city to Spain?

   _____

3. What other acts were part of the formal ceremony? _____

   _____

CHAPTER REVIEW: CRITICAL THINKING

Countries often gave land to other countries when they lost wars or when one country became weak and the other grew stronger. People living in those territories had little to say about the change in government. When Spain took over Louisiana, the people in the colony were governed by those who spoke a different language and had different laws. Yet people had to obey their new rulers. Sometimes you can learn **different points of view** by trying to understand why people acted as they did.

1. How would you feel if a country with a different language and laws took over your

   country? _____

   _____

2. Do you think the French rebels in Louisiana in 1768 were right or wrong to claim that they

   had a right to choose their own government? Explain. _____

   _____

10 18th CENTURY SPANISH EXPLORERS

AIMS: What new areas did Spanish explorers find in the 18th century? What led them to discover these areas?

1. Beginning in 1691 and on into the early 1700s, Eusebio Kino, a Jesuit priest, explored the desert areas of the Southwest. He built missions in Arizona. He made several expeditions into nearby areas, including Baja California. Spanish explorers who came after Kino depended on the maps Kino made of the area.

2. In the mid-1700s, the Spanish began to worry about Russians exploring the northwest coast. The Spanish wanted to protect Spanish claims to the region. Spain sent Juan Pérez in 1774 to investigate. He sailed from Monterey up the Pacific coast , but bad weather forced him to turn back. Pérez returned to the northwest coast the next year. Pérez, Bruno de Heceta, and Juan Francisco de la Bodega explored what is now northern Oregon and southern Washington. They found the mouth of the Columbia River. They reached the coast of British Columbia and took possession of this territory for Spain. Bodega and Pérez explored the coast of Alaska from 1774 to 1775.

3. At about the same time, Juan Bautista de Anza wanted to find a good land route between Arizona and California. He reached San Gabriel Mission in California in 1774 and continued to Monterey before returning to Arizona. On Anza's second trip in 1775, he brought soldiers and their wives, missionaries, and other settlers. They crossed the Colorado River and built a cabin for missionaries at what is now Yuma, Arizona. During the trip to Monterey, eight babies were born. The first child born in California of Spanish parents was born on Christmas Eve, 1775. Anza went on to set up the mission and presidio of San Francisco de Asís. It was the beginning of the city of San Francisco.

4. Silvestre Vélez de Escalante, a Franciscan missionary, looked for a trail west from Santa Fe to Monterey in 1776. He took along Bernardo Miera, a mapmaker. Heavy snow kept them from reaching California, but their 2,000-mile trip took them into western Colorado, central and eastern Utah, and northern Arizona. They were the first known Europeans to see these lands. Miera's maps and Escalante's journal gave a good record of their trip.

5. In 1789, Alejandro Malaspina sailed from Spain on a scientific voyage. He took along geographers, scientists, nature experts, and artists. After traveling in South America, Malaspina began a search for a northwest passage that would give ships a water route between the Pacific and Atlantic oceans. Legends told of a **strait**, a narrow waterway connecting two large bodies of water, that might lead to such a passage. This strait was supposed to be on the coast of Alaska or British Columbia.

6. Malaspina sailed north in May 1790 to avoid ice blocking the water. In a small boat, Malaspina reached an inlet in Alaska that seemed to be the strait. Finally, he reached a glacier, now known as Malaspina Glacier. He could go no farther by water, but he gave Spain its most northern claim to land on the West Coast.

▲ Eusebio Kino, a Jesuit missionary, went on 40 expeditions into Arizona. He opposed the use of Native American as slaves in northern Mexican silver mines.

Understanding What You Have Read

Write the names of the persons below next to the statement that each might have made.

Juan Bautista de Anza   Juan de la Bodega   Eusebio Kino
Silvestre Vélez de Escalante   Alejandro Malaspina   Juan Pérez

_____ 1. I explored desert areas of the Southwest at the end of the 17th century.

_____ 2. I explored northern Oregon and southern Washington.

_____ 3. I sailed into southern Alaska in 1775.

_____ 4. I founded what is now Yuma in Arizona, and San Francisco in California.

_____ 5. I led the first Europeans into Utah and western Colorado.

_____ 6. I sailed farther north than any other Spanish explorer. An Alaskan glacier is named after me.

Linking Past to Present

Read the following passage. Then answer the questions.

Spanish Trails and Ports. Many of the trails that were blazed across the United States by the early Spanish explorers are routes used today. The old Camino Real in California runs along today's U. S. 101. The Camino Real established a route between settlements. Other modern highways have been built along the routes of old Spanish roads.

The Spanish explorers and settlers also found and developed many of the important ocean and river ports. In Florida, they developed St. Augustine. In New Orleans, Governor Ulloa enlarged a shipping channel at the mouth of the Mississippi River. Spanish explorers also developed harbors at San Diego, Monterey, and San Francisco.

▲ Pictured above is the city of New Orleans during the 18th century.

1. Today Route 101 in California runs along the path of the old _____.

2. An important harbor the early Spanish developed in California was

_____.

3. The Spanish governor in New Orleans enlarged a channel of the _____ River.

4. Are there any roads or ports in your state that were started by early Spanish, French, British, or other colonists or by Native Americans? Name one and write who started it:

_____

Alejandro Malaspina. Alejandro Malaspina dreamed of sailing around the world and making scientific discoveries. He planned a voyage that would provide new scientific knowledge. He also wanted to help Spain politically. He left Spain for the Americas in 1789. His ships, *Descubierta* ("Discovery") and *Atrevida* ("Daring"), had the most up-to-date scientific instruments of the time. José Bustamante went along as his second in command.

Malaspina stopped along the coasts of Chile and Peru. The scientists he brought along studied the coastal waters, the mountains, and the Amazon jungle.

Early in 1790, Malaspina received new orders from Spain. He was told to look for a route between the Pacific and Atlantic oceans. Malaspina left many of his scientists and artists in South America to continue their work. He took along only a third of his people.

Once Malaspina and Bustamante reached the northwest coast of North America, they set out in small boats to explore. It was extremely dangerous along the rocky coast. Glaciers threatened them. When Malaspina and Bustamante finally found what they thought was the strait they were looking for, it was hard to navigate. Finally, they arrived at an enormous glacier. A member of the crew climbed up and reported that there was no water route.

Malaspina was discouraged, but on the trip back he explored the coast carefully. Although he did not find what he wanted, he was the first to have the area mapped. He claimed for Spain land that was far north on the Pacific coast of North America.

Recalling the Facts

Choose each correct answer and write the letter in the space provided.

_____ 1. Alejandro Malaspina dreamed of
   a. discovering Alaska.
   b. sailing around the world.
   c. settling in Peru.

_____ 2. Malaspina's ships carried
   a. settlers for the New World.
   b. sailors to fight Britain.
   c. up-to-date scientific instruments.

_____ 3. Malaspina changed his plans because
   a. Spain sent him new orders.
   b. he got tired of the rainy season.
   c. his scientists wanted to stay in South America.

_____ 4. When he sailed north, Malaspina wanted to find
   a. a glacier in Alaska.
   b. a way to map the northwest coast.
   c. a route between the Atlantic and Pacific oceans.

_____ 5. Malaspina made the trip worthwhile by
   a. naming all the places.
   b. being the first to see Washington and Oregon.
   c. having maps made of the area he explored.

The Arts and Technology

Dress and Costume. The Spanish were very careful about differences in social classes. One way they showed class differences was by the way they dressed.

The rich in the New World wore very fancy outfits of silk and velvet. Men wore bright-colored jackets and silk sashes. Their trousers were of velvet and their shoes were often embroidered. Men sometimes also wore a **sarape**, a colorful blanket carried on one shoulder. Women wore silk dresses with lace trim. Women also wore a **rebozo**, a long shawl of fine material with silk fringe. They sometimes wore pearls and fine jewels.

Whenever possible, wealthy people wore clothing from Europe. Even the most beautiful hand-woven wools were not considered good enough if they were made locally.

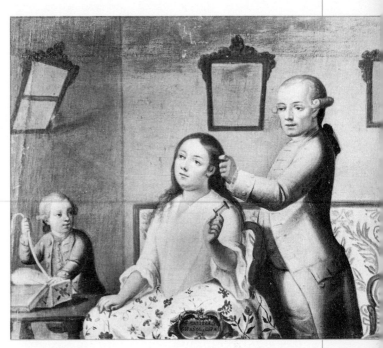

Do you think that the family in this picture was wealthy? Why? _____

_____

CHAPTER REVIEW: CRITICAL THINKING

One way to **summarize** information is to make a chart that puts important facts into **categories**. This chart has three categories: Name, Dates, Accomplishments. Complete the chart. Then write a one- or two-sentence **generalization** based on the information in the chart.

Name	Dates	Accomplishments
Eusebio Kino	1691–1711	
Juan Pérez		Explored the northwest coast including the coast of British Columbia and Alaska
Juan Bautista de Anza		
	1776	Explored and mapped western Colorado and parts of Utah and Arizona
	1790	Explored and did scientific research along the Alaskan coast

Generalization: _____

_____

Chapter 11

DAILY LIFE IN THE SPANISH COLONIES

AIMS: How did the Spanish shape the style of living in North America? What was life like for Native Americans under the Spanish?

1. Spanish settlers wanted their colonies in the New World to be like Spain. They even called part of their North and Central American empire New Spain. The Spanish brought their language, customs, and religion. They changed the lives of the Native Americans they met, but their own lives changed, too.

2. The mission was the most important means of bringing Spanish culture to the New World. A mission was a school, farm, church, and center of community life. Life at missions was similar, no matter where the mission was. Priests taught the local Native Americans reading, writing, arithmetic, and religion. Usually, a presidio, or fort, with Spanish soldiers was near the mission. Small pueblos, or communities, of Spanish settlers grew around successful missions.

3. Each day at a mission began with religious services. Marriages and other ceremonies took place at the morning service. After breakfast, the Native Americans worked on the mission land, took time for lunch, and then continued working until dinner. In the evenings when there was no work, there might be dancing, singing, and games.

4. The main job for Native American men and boys was farming. They raised European crops, such as wheat and rice, and American crops, such as **maize** (corn), beans, and squash. They also herded the sheep and cattle that the Spanish brought. Native American women learned crafts and cooked. Soon a new style of cooking mixed European and Native American ways of preparing food.

5. A class system in the New World was based on people's background. At the top were *peninsulares*, people born in Spain of Spanish parents. The children of Spanish parents born in the Americas were *criollos*. Even if they came from important Spanish families, *criollos* got fewer important jobs than people born in Spain. *Mestizos* came next. *Mestizos* were people who had mixed Spanish and Native American background. The Native Americans came last, except if the community had blacks. In that case free blacks came next and black slaves last.

6. Different Spanish colonies had different ways of life. In the 1600s, St. Augustine, Florida, had farming and cattle ranching. There was also danger. The community had to protect itself from pirate raids and other attacks. When Great Britain occupied Florida in 1763, the mission system and the mission way of life ended. Most Spanish settlers moved to Cuba.

7. Apache and Comanche attacks were the main problem for the people of San Antonio. In the 1720s, that town had about 200 Spanish and Mexicans. Within a few decades, San Antonio had grown to about 4,000 settlers, and 1,000 were soldiers. Most Spanish settlers lived by hunting, fishing, and farming. They also raised some sheep and cattle.

▲ People of mixed Spanish and Native American background were called *mestizos*.

Complete each of the following sentences. Then find each word in the word puzzle. The hidden words are spelled from top to bottom, left to right, and diagonally (from corner to corner). Circle the words as you find them. The first one has been done for you.

1. Native Americans grew maize, which is also known as _____.

2. A military fort built by the Spanish was called a _____.

3. A community that grew around a successful mission was a _____.

4. A religious settlement set up to teach Native Americans and to convert them to Christianity was called a _____.

5. People living in the Americas but born in Spain of Spanish parents were called _____.

6. People born in the Americas of Spanish parents were called _____.

7. People who had one Spanish and one Native American parent were called _____.

C	B	U	M	A	Y	W	C	E	A	P	M
A	D	C	R	I	O	L	L	O	S	U	E
P	E	N	I	N	S	U	L	A	R	E	S
E	V	C	E	I	F	S	E	Q	U	B	T
U	T	O	Y	C	O	X	I	D	F	L	I
T	P	R	E	S	I	D	I	O	G	O	Z
U	H	N	I	L	H	U	Z	M	N	Y	O
S	T	L	B	A	C	K	O	C	D	E	S

Linking Past to Present

Read the following passage. Then write the word or words that best complete each sentence.

Creole. The word *Creole* started out meaning a person of European parents who was born in the New World. The Spanish word *criollo* first meant a person born in the New World of Spanish parents. In Louisiana, a Creole was someone born of French parents. These were the main meanings for the word in the early period of Spanish settlement. Today, the meaning of the word *Creole* depends on where it is used.

In Louisiana, a Creole is a person whose ancestors were the early French settlers. In the states along the Gulf of Mexico, a Creole is a person whose ancestors were among the early Spanish settlers. In the West Indies and some other places, a Creole is usually a person with European and African ancestors.

It is important to remember that each place has its own meaning for the word. When you use the word *Creole*, you have to know what it means in a particular place.

1. The Spanish word *criollo* first meant a person born of _____ in the New World.

2. In Louisiana, Creoles are people whose ancestors were _____.

3. In the West Indies, Creoles have both European and _____ ancestors.

4. In the _____ states, a Creole is a person whose ancestors were among the early Spanish settlers.

Spotlight on People

Laureano de Torres y Ayala. The first of four Cuban-born governors of La Florida was Laureano de Torres y Ayala. In 1693, when Torres became governor, La Florida included the present states of Florida, Georgia, Alabama, and parts of South Carolina and Mississippi.

Torres was born in Havana, Cuba, in 1645. He had served honorably in the Spanish army.

When Torres arrived in St. Augustine, he faced threats from the British in Charleston, South Carolina. The British and their Native American allies destroyed a Native American village and kidnapped Native Americans. The British then had the Apalachicola Indians attack the Spanish mission of San Carlos. They robbed the church and took 42 Christian Indians as slaves. In return, Governor Torres sent soldiers to burn several Apalachicola villages.

Despite a shortage of money and many difficulties, Torres strengthened Spanish defenses. He saw the Castillo de San Marcos completed in 1695. He worked on a sea wall to protect St. Augustine from floods. He also built a fort at San Luis de Talimali, the largest and most important mission in La Florida. About 1,400 Native Americans lived there together with Franciscan missionaries and Spanish soldiers.

After completing his term as governor, Torres went to Spain and fought in a war. He was promoted to marshal of the army. He served as governor of Cuba from 1708 to 1711 and again from 1713 to 1716.

Laureano de Torres y Ayala earned the title of Marquis de Casa Torres for his success in buying tobacco for the Spanish Royal Treasury. He died in Havana in 1722.

Recalling the Facts

Choose each correct answer and write the letter in the space provided.

_____ 1. Laureano de Torres y Ayala was born in
   a. Florida.
   b. Cuba.
   c. Spain.

_____ 2. In 1693, Torres became
   a. a general in the army.
   b. governor of La Florida.
   c. governor of Cuba.

_____ 3. When Torres arrived, he faced the problem of
   a. raids by Apalachicola Indians and the British.
   b. building the San Carlos mission.
   c. destroying the San Luis mission.

_____ 4. While governor, Torres
   a. began building the Castillo de San Marcos.
   b. completed the Castillo de San Marcos.
   c. destroyed the Castillo de San Marcos.

_____ 5. Much of Torres's work in La Florida helped
   a. make peace with the British.
   b. make peace with the Native Americans.
   c. make Spanish settlements stronger.

_____ 6. One of Torres's jobs after leaving La Florida was
   a. viceroy of New Spain.
   b. admiral of the Spanish navy.
   c. governor of Cuba.

Using Primary Sources

Sor Juana Inés de la Cruz (1651–1695). Juana Inés de Asbaje (her original name) became one of the greatest poets of New Spain. She was born in a Mexican village and learned to read at the age of three. By the time she was eight, she was writing poetry. She wanted to enter the University of Mexico, but was forbidden because she was not a boy. At nine, she moved to Mexico City. Her fame as a poet and scholar spread. She was invited to the court of the viceroy of New Spain. There her intelligence, talent, and beauty made her famous. Sor Juana Inés de la Cruz became a nun. She sold the books she owned and gave the money to the poor.

Read this section of her poem "To Hope." Then answer the questions.

> Green spellbinder [smooth talker] of human life,
> crazy hope, gilded frenzy [wildness painted with fake gold],
> what men dream of when they are awake, confused,
> as in a dream, worthless in her treasures;
>
> Let them follow your [hope's] name in search of your light
> those who wear green spectacles [eyeglasses]
> and see everything painted as they wish it;
>
> But I, wise in my fortune,
> keep both my eyes in my two hands
> and see only what I touch.

Did Sor Juana Inés de la Cruz describe hope as a good or bad feeling to have? Do you think her viewpoint is common to other periods of history? Explain. _____

_____

_____

CHAPTER REVIEW: CRITICAL THINKING

Spain organized its colonies in the same way in each part of its empire. Yet by the 17th and 18th centuries, each Spanish colony began to develop its own way of life. Different **causes** resulted in different **effects**.

List two differences in the history or geography of the Spanish colonies that might help explain some differences in their way of life. _____

_____

_____

12 THE AMERICAN REVOLUTION

AIM: How did Spain and its colonies help America during the American Revolution?

1. The American colonies declared their independence from Great Britain in 1776. To win their war against Great Britain, they needed help from other countries such as France. Spain and its colonies also came to the aid of the Americans.

2. Help came in several forms. Spain and its colonies gave money and supplies. Many Spanish, Cuban, Mexican, Puerto Rican, Dominican, and Venezuelan soldiers fought and died in battles against the British.

3. In 1779, Spain declared war against Great Britain. Spain was still angry about losing Florida in 1763. One of Spain's aims was to get back Florida from the British. The Spanish also wanted to drive the British out of the Gulf of Mexico and the Caribbean.

4. Representatives from Spain and France met to decide how to help the 13 colonies. Each country gave a great amount of money to the Americans. Spain continued to send money to the 13 colonies throughout the American Revolution. A Spanish company shipped weapons, ammunition, and supplies. Spain also let Americans use ports in Spain and its colonies.

5. Diego de Gardoqui, a wealthy Spanish banker, helped the Spanish government send money to the Americans. His assistance continued until the end of the war. After America became independent, Gardoqui served as Spain's ambassador to the United States.

6. The Spanish colonies also helped. Bernardo de Gálvez, the governor of Louisiana, provided gunpowder, guns, food, medicine, and other supplies to the Americans fighting in the West. In California, Father Junípero Serra collected money from both Spanish settlers and Native Americans.

7. Juan Manuel de Cagigal was governor of Cuba during the American Revolution. Many people who had left La Florida when Great Britain took over in 1763 were now living in Cuba. Cagigal and his assistant Francisco de Miranda got Cubans to give a great deal of financial help. Most of the Cuban money was collected from the wealthy women of Havana. They gave their jewelry and diamonds to help the Americans. The millions of dollars worth of money raised in Havana went to General George Washington and General Rochambeau, the French commander. This money was crucial in preparing for the last battle of the American Revolution in Yorktown. One reason the Cubans helped was that they hated the British for the suffering caused by the British capture of Havana in 1762. Cuba also let American ships dock in Havana without charge. They repaired the ships at no cost.

8. Spain did not officially recognize United States independence until after the war. However, it did send representatives to the 13 colonies. Juan de Miralles and his secretary, Francisco Rendón, traveled through the colonies. They discussed trade and assistance from Spain. Miralles helped gain the freedom of both Spanish colonists and Americans who were captured by the British during the war.

GOLFO DE MEXICO

▲ Spanish ships attack the British during the American Revolution. Spanish-speaking soldiers from what areas fought against the British?

Match the people listed in Column A with the way they helped the American Revolution, as described in Column B.

Column A		Column B
_____ 1. wealthy women of Havana	a.	collected money in California for the Americans
_____ 2. Diego de Gardoqui	b.	provided supplies for Americans fighting in the West
_____ 3. Bernardo de Gálvez	c.	gained freedom for prisoners of war
_____ 4. Junípero Serra	d.	banker who helped transfer money from Spain to the colonies
_____ 5. Juan de Cagigal	e.	gave diamonds and jewels for the American Revolution
_____ 6. Juan de Miralles	f.	as governor, encouraged Cubans to help the colonists

Linking Past to Present

Study the time line. Then complete each of the following sentences.

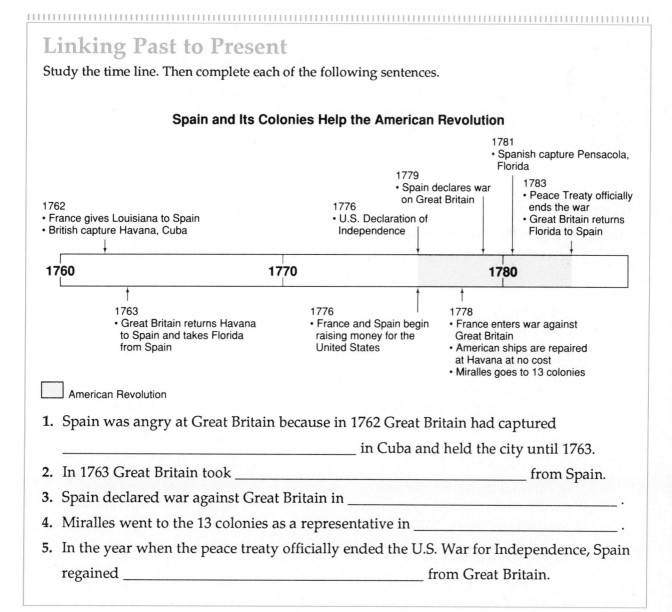

Spain and Its Colonies Help the American Revolution

1762
• France gives Louisiana to Spain
• British capture Havana, Cuba

1763
• Great Britain returns Havana to Spain and takes Florida from Spain

1776
• U.S. Declaration of Independence

1776
• France and Spain begin raising money for the United States

1779
• Spain declares war on Great Britain

1778
• France enters war against Great Britain
• American ships are repaired at Havana at no cost
• Miralles goes to 13 colonies

1781
• Spanish capture Pensacola, Florida

1783
• Peace Treaty officially ends the war
• Great Britain returns Florida to Spain

1760   1770   1780

☐ American Revolution

1. Spain was angry at Great Britain because in 1762 Great Britain had captured

_____ in Cuba and held the city until 1763.

2. In 1763 Great Britain took _____ from Spain.

3. Spain declared war against Great Britain in _____ .

4. Miralles went to the 13 colonies as a representative in _____ .

5. In the year when the peace treaty officially ended the U.S. War for Independence, Spain

regained _____ from Great Britain.

Spotlight on People

Juan de Miralles. Juan de Miralles was a strong supporter of the United States War for Independence. Born in Spain, Miralles moved to Cuba when he was young. He married the daughter of an important Cuban family and became a wealthy merchant. He spoke English and French as well as Spanish.

When Miralles was in his sixties, he was asked to serve as a Spanish agent and observer in the 13 colonies. He reported to the captain general of Cuba and the minister of the Indies in Spain.

In 1778, Miralles landed at Charleston, South Carolina, with his secretary, Francisco Rendón. They traveled to other cities in the colonies. In each city, Miralles discussed increasing Cuban trade with the United States.

Besides improving trade between the colonial cities and Cuba, Miralles helped to free some of the Spanish and Americans who were captured by the British during the Revolution. He also tried to get the Continental Congress to raise an army to attack the British forces in Florida.

Miralles met most of the revolutionary leaders and members of the Continental Congress. Before long, he and George Washington became good friends. Miralles encouraged Spain to declare war against Great Britain.

Miralles also contributed his own money for the American Revolution. He helped pay for the repairs for a fleet of seven ships of Commodore Alexander Gillon of South Carolina. The ships were repaired in the Havana shipyards.

When Miralles became seriously ill, both George and Martha Washington helped look after him. After Miralles died, his secretary, Francisco Rendón, continued to represent Spain in the 13 colonies. George Washington, himself, presided at Miralles's funeral.

Recalling the Facts

Choose each correct answer and write the letter in the space provided.

_____ 1. Juan de Miralles lived most of his life in
   a. Cuba.
   b. Spain
   c. South Carolina.

_____ 2. Spain sent Miralles to the 13 colonies as
   a. an ambassador.
   b. captain general of Cuba.
   c. an observer and agent.

_____ 3. In each colonial city Miralles went to, he
   a. needed translators for English.
   b. tried to improve trade with Cuba.
   c. supplied soldiers.

_____ 4. Another way Miralles helped was by
   a. attacking Florida.
   b. getting prisoners freed.
   c. stopping trade with Cuba.

_____ 5. Miralles wanted Congress to
   a. vote for money for Cuba.
   b. set Spaniards free.
   c. attack the British in Florida.

_____ 6. George Washington
   a. never got to meet Miralles.
   b. knew Miralles slightly.
   c. was a good friend who helped when Miralles was sick.

Using Primary Sources

After Juan de Miralles died, George Washington wrote a letter, dated April 30, 1780, to Marshal Diego Navarro, the captain general of Cuba. Read the part of the letter printed below. Then answer the questions that follow.

> . . . Your Excellency will have the goodness to believe, that I took pleasure in performing every friendly office to him during his illness, and that no care or attention in our power was omitted toward his comfort or restoration. I the more sincerely sympathize with you in the loss of so estimable a friend, as, ever since his residence with us, I have been happy in ranking him among the number of mine. It must, however, be some consolation to his connections [relatives] to know that in this country he has been universally regretted [missed].

1. What phrase or phrases show that Washington considered Miralles a good friend?

   _____

   _____

2. According to Washington, how did Americans feel about Miralles's death?

   _____

   _____

CHAPTER REVIEW: CRITICAL THINKING

Why did Spain, which had its own colonies, help the 13 British colonies in the American War for Independence? After all, that war might have given people in the Spanish colonies the idea of fighting for their own independence from Spain. Spain's leaders looked at the **alternatives**, or different choices they had. Then they made what they thought was the right **decision**. However, within 50 years, most of Spain's New World colonies were free of Spain.

Spain and Great Britain were bitter enemies since Great Britain had captured Havana in 1762. The Spanish had to give La Florida to Great Britain in 1763 in order to get Havana back. Spain did get Florida back in 1783 after Great Britain lost the American War for Independence.

If you were the king of Spain in the 1770s, would you have helped the 13 British colonies in their fight against Great Britain? Give reasons for your decision.

_____

_____

_____

_____

13 SPANISH HEROES IN THE REVOLUTION

AIM: How did Spanish military efforts help the Thirteen Colonies win their fight for independence?

1. Many Hispanics helped fight the British during the American Revolution. Spanish-born Jorge Ferragut fought in both the Continental Navy and Army. As a naval officer, he fought in the Battle of Savannah in 1779. He was captured in Charleston. After Ferragut was freed, he joined the Continental army and earned the rank of major.

2. Another Spaniard who helped the American Revolution was the governor of Louisiana, Bernardo de Gálvez. He opened the port of New Orleans to American ships, captured British ships, and ordered British subjects to leave Louisiana. Gálvez also sent money, gunpowder, and supplies to American troops in the Ohio Valley and the army of General Washington in Virginia.

3. After Spain declared war against Great Britain in 1779, Gálvez attacked British forts along the Mississippi River. In September 1779, the Spanish captured the British forts at Manchac, Baton Rouge, and Natchez. In a few weeks, Gálvez had captured the British forts along the east bank of the lower Mississippi. He took more than 1,000 prisoners. In February 1780, Spanish forces captured the British fort of St. Joseph on Lake Michigan. By early 1780, they had destroyed British rule on the Mississippi.

4. Gálvez also attacked the British ports along the coast of the Gulf of Mexico. In January 1780, he left New Orleans with an army of 754 men. Joining Gálvez at Mobile were 567 troops from Cuba. After a short battle, Gálvez captured Mobile. He left Colonel José de Ezpeleta in charge there. When British and Native American forces tried to retake Mobile, Ezpeleta defeated them.

5. Gálvez then set out to capture Pensacola, the main British base in West Florida. Pensacola had two strong forts and an island that made it difficult to sail safely into the Bay of Pensacola.

6. Gálvez went to Havana to get additional troops and ships. When he tried to return to Florida, weather and other problems made the Spanish turn back to Cuba. They left Havana on February 28, 1781. Gálvez had an army of 7,000 men from Cuba, Mexico, Santo Domingo, Haiti, Venezuela, and New Orleans.

7. Juan Manuel de Cagigal was the field marshal commanding the additional army troops that arrived from Havana to help Gálvez at Pensacola. Admiral José Solano took charge of shipping Cagigal and his army to Pensacola. Solano had helped build up the Spanish navy after years of neglect. José de Ezpeleta and his troops from Mobile also helped Gálvez at Pensacola.

8. To begin his attack, Gálvez led a small party onto Santa Rosa Island, which guards Pensacola Bay. Then he sailed into Pensacola Bay. The Spanish ferried troops from the island to the mainland. On May 8, a Spanish shell set fire to the British powder storage. On May 10, 1781, the British surrendered. Over 1,000 British were taken prisoner. The British had lost all their defenses on the Gulf of Mexico and the Mississippi River. Many historians believe that Gálvez's victory made the American victory at Yorktown possible.

▲ Bernardo de Gálvez leads the Spanish troops at the Battle of Pensacola.

Understanding What You Have Read

Write the names of the persons below next to the statement that each might have made.

Bernardo de Gálvez   Juan de Cagigal   Jorge Ferragut
José de Ezpeleta   José Solano

_____ **1.** I was governor of Louisiana and drove the British out of the Mississippi area and the Gulf of Mexico.

_____ **2.** I fought in the Continental navy and army.

_____ **3.** I kept the British from retaking Mobile and then marched troops to Pensacola.

_____ **4.** I was in charge of the army troops that helped Gálvez at Pensacola.

_____ **5.** I was in charge of shipping troops from Havana to Pensacola.

Building Geography Skills

Study the map. Then answer the questions.

1. Who owned Florida during the Revolution?

   _____

2. What were two of the British-held seaports along the Gulf Coast that Spanish troops attacked?

   _____

   _____

3. A British fort near the Great Lakes was captured by Spanish forces. What was the name of this fort?

   _____

4. How many miles inland from the Gulf of Mexico did the Spanish troops get during the Revolution?

   _____

5. The British at Mobile were attacked by Spanish troops from the city of

   _____.

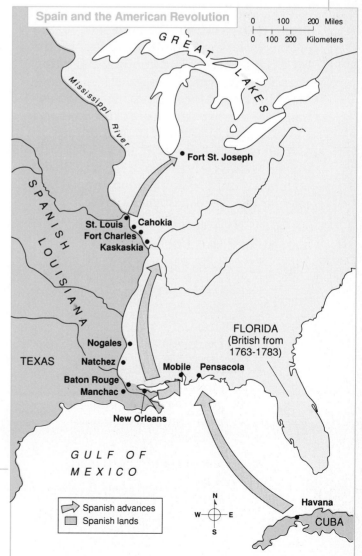

Spain and the American Revolution

Bernardo de Gálvez. The hero of the Battle of Pensacola was Bernardo de Gálvez He led his troops bravely and continued fighting after being wounded. The Americans recognized his importance by making his descendants eligible to be members of the Sons and Daughters of the American Revolution.

Gálvez was born in Spain in 1746. His uncle José de Gálvez was in charge of the Spanish colonies. His uncle encouraged him to enter the Spanish Royal Guards.

After fighting in Europe in the Seven Years' War, Gálvez was promoted and sent to New Spain to fight the Apaches. Later he wrote a guide on dealing fairly with the Native Americans.

He returned to Spain and then went to France, where he studied military science. In 1776, he went to New Orleans as a lieutenant colonel. A short time later, he became governor of Louisiana. There he met and married Félicie de Maxent d'Estréhan, a widow from a well-known French family.

Gálvez planned the Battle of Pensacola. He was wounded, but he kept fighting. He led his troops when other officers refused to fight. After a brief fight, the British surrendered to the Spanish.

In recognition of the bravery of Bernardo de Gálvez, King Charles III of Spain issued a royal proclamation. In it, he noted some of the brave deeds Gálvez had accomplished. The king named Pensacola Bay the Bahía de Santa María de Gálvez. In addition, the king made Gálvez a count and gave him the right to use the words *Yo solo*, "I alone," on his coat of arms. Gálvez also became governor and captain general of the newly created provinces of Louisiana and West Florida. In 1785, he became viceroy of New Spain. He died in 1786 in Mexico.

Recalling the Facts

Choose each correct answer and write the letter in the space provided.

_____ 1. Bernardo de Gálvez was born in
   a. Spain.
   b. Cuba.
   c. Louisiana.

_____ 2. Gálvez's uncle was
   a. governor of Cuba.
   b. governor of La Florida.
   c. in charge of the Spanish colonies.

_____ 3. Gálvez went to Louisiana in 1776 as
   a. governor.
   b. leader of a missionary group.
   c. lieutenant colonel.

_____ 4. During the Battle of Pensacola, Gálvez
   a. planned attacks but did not fight.
   b. kept fighting after being wounded.
   c. surrendered to the British.

_____ 5. King Charles III
   a. issued a royal proclamation praising Gálvez.
   b. did not promote Gálvez.
   c. ordered Gálvez to return to Spain and fight in Europe.

Using Primary Sources

Bernardo de Gálvez kept a diary of the events of the Battle of Pensacola. In it, he refers to himself as "the general." Read the following items from his diary. Then write the answers to the questions that follow.

[April] The eleventh, a deserter arrived with the news that the [Spanish soldier] who had gone over to the enemy had informed [the British general] that the army was composed of 3,000 men. [The British general] expected a reinforcement of Indians and considerable aid from Jamaica. [T]he day before [the British general] had written to Georgia also [asking for] help in driving us out of the country.

At four the advanced guards advised that several [British] troops came out from [the fort] . . . perhaps to attack us from several sides; in a little while several bands of Indians came forward and began their fire against [our troops]. . . .

[We] returned the fire of the Indians and the English. . . .

A quarter of an hour after this the general received the information that the enemy was approaching from three different sides with two small cannon. . . . [He] went forward to inspect the place where they were headed and to cut off their retreat. . . . [H]aving arrived . . . he received a bullet which went through a finger of his left hand and made a furrow in his abdomen, for which reason he retired to his tent so that the surgeons could give him first aid. . . . [The general ordered] Major General Ezpeleta to take over from him immediately . . . until his wounds would permit him to attend to all of it again.

---

1. What information did General Gálvez get from the British deserter? _____

   _____

2. Give an example of a risk that General Gálvez took with his own safety. _____

   _____

CHAPTER REVIEW: CRITICAL THINKING

Wars are fought on several **fronts,** or areas of fighting. Soldiers, weapons, food, and supplies are needed at each front. Most of the colonial troops were fighting in the 13 colonies. The Spanish forces were fighting outside the area of the 13 colonies.

How can we easily understand how important a historical event is? One way is by trying to imagine what would have happened if that important event had not occurred. Use your imagination to **predict,** or make a guess about, what might have happened in these examples:

1. On what other fronts might the 13 colonies have had to fight if the Spanish had not battled

   the British?_____

   _____

2. Do you think that the United States could have won its independence when it did without

   the help of Spain and France? Explain._____

   _____

14 DAILY LIFE IN SPANISH AMERICA AFTER 1783

AIMS: How did life in Spanish America change after the American Revolution? Why did the changes take place?

1. For 20 years after 1763, the British occupied and colonized Florida. They built roads and buildings. During the American Revolution, St. Augustine was a depot for British troops and a haven for Tories. It was also a center for prisoners of war. In 1783, as part of the treaty that ended the war, Florida was returned to Spain.

2. Many Spanish settlers returned in the summer of 1784 with the new governor, Vicente Manuel de Zéspedes y Velasco. There were more than a thousand settlers and soldiers. A small group had lived in Florida before. A few had remained during the British rule.

3. The streets of St. Augustine echoed with sounds of many languages. The people of St.

Augustine came from different cultures. The largest group of settlers came from Minorca, a Spanish island that had been taken by Great Britain, then France, and returned to Spain in 1783. Many settlers were not Spanish. They came from Italy, Greece, Switzerland, Germany, and other parts of Europe. Some Blacks in St. Augustine were free, but most were slaves.

4. Father Thomas Hassett, born in Ireland and educated in Spain, set up the first integrated public school in St. Augustine in 1787. The first teacher of this school was Father Francisco Traconis, who was from Santiago de Cuba. The school lasted until 1821, when Spain again lost control of Florida, this time to the United States.

5. In St. Augustine, as in all of the Spanish colonies, religious holidays were important times. They were times in which the entire community celebrated.

6. In the Southwest, a big change was happening in cattle raising. The change began in Mexico around 1750. Owners let their cattle roam on the range, and then gathered them each year to brand them. Large ranchos were being started. They had thousand of acres and were owned by wealthy rancheros.

7. The new method of large-scale cattle ranching began in the south, at the Rio Grande border around 1750. In the early 1800s, it spread north to Texas. In the 19th century, it would become a way of life throughout the Southwest. Ranchos were also found in California.

8. Vaqueros, or cowboys, developed many skills. Most of their work was done on horseback. They would hold contests to see who was the best rider or cattle roper. Rodeos developed from these contests.

9. While these changes were taking place, another change was coming. Americans from the new United States were beginning to move west into lands that belonged to Spain.

▲ Native Americans are being taught at a mission school in the Southwest.

Fill in the best word or phrase for each statement.

1. The largest group of people who settled in Florida after 1783 came from _____.

2. Father Thomas Hassett started an _____ in St. Augustine.

3. The Spanish had to leave Florida again in _____.

4. The new method of large-scale cattle ranching moved into Texas from _____.

5. The _____ came from contests of cowboy skills.

Linking Past to Present

Vaqueros and Cowboys. The beginnings of the American cowboy really started in the Mexican part of New Spain and spread northward. A great deal of the customs, the language, and the style of clothes came from vaqueros who had begun to ranch in the new style.

Ranchers and cowboys wore big, wide-brimmed hats called *sombreros.* The hats protected them from sun, wind, and rain. The cowboys also protected their legs with *chaparreras,* or **chaps.** They wore leather belts, boots, and jackets. Those who had the money decorated their clothing with silver buckles and buttons. The main tool for roping cattle was *la reata,* which became **lariat** or *reata* in English. Even the style of roping cattle came from the Mexican part of New Spain.

The cattle and horses were rounded up and kept in **corrals.** That word comes from a Spanish word meaning "ring" or "circle." The wild horses, or **broncos,** got their name from a Spanish word meaning "rough."

Label this diagram by writing the correct word in the space provided.

▲ Zéspedes lived in the Governor's House, one of the main buildings in St. Augustine.

Vincente Manuel de Zéspedes. Spain gained control of Florida again in 1783. In 1784, Vincente Manuel de Zéspedes arrived from Havana to become governor. With him were 500 soldiers and two Catholic priests. A third priest joined them later.

Governor Zéspedes began dealing with the colony's problems. Two problems he faced were controlling the bandits that roamed the country and treating Blacks fairly.

He had the most noted bandits caught and sent to jail in Havana. Then he let people know that the government would protect the rights of free Blacks if the Blacks could prove they were free. There were Black men and officers in the regiments, as well.

The colony had people from many lands. Governor Zéspedes hoped to make the colony able to support itself. In 1787, he wrote a letter to the government of Spain telling how Florida could be developed. One idea was to let people from the United States move to Florida. Spain did not like his plan. It did not think Florida was worth developing. Yet in that year, non-Spanish, non-Catholic settlers were allowed in.

When Charles IV became king of Spain in 1788, Governor Zéspedes held a three-day festival to celebrate the event. There were parades, portraits of the king, the sounds of guns and church bells, and plays. Shortly after, the king and queen had a daughter, and another celebration followed.

The governor's health was poor. He asked to be moved to another post. He left Florida in 1790.

Recalling the Facts

Choose each correct answer and write the letter in the space provided.

_____ 1. Zéspedes went to Florida to
   a. become governor.
   b. take over the army.
   c. free black slaves.

_____ 2. One problem the governor had to solve was
   a. getting army support.
   b. removing black settlers.
   c. arresting bandits.

_____ 3. Zéspedes hoped that Florida would
   a. become British.
   b. keep out foreigners.
   c. be able to support itself.

_____ 4. Zéspedes suggested that Spain should
   a. allow people from the United States to settle in Florida.
   b. not allow the colony to grow any larger.
   c. join the United States.

_____ 5. Governor Zéspedes held a festival
   a. in honor of his anniversary.
   b. because he was leaving.
   c. to celebrate a new king.

_____ 6. Zéspedes left Florida because
   a. the king dismissed him.
   b. the king wanted him in Spain.
   c. his health was bad.

Using Primary Sources

Here are some of the rules that governed the first integrated public school in the United States at St. Augustine, Florida. Read the rules. Then answer the questions that follow.

> 5. Throughout the year the schools shall be opened at seven o'clock in the morning and at two in the afternoon. At no time shall the pupils be dismissed in the morning before twelve o'clock, nor in the afternoon in winter before sunset. . . .
>
> 10. The school rooms shall be swept at least once a week by the pupils. . . .
>
> 12. . . . [T]o the first or most capable of each class shall be given some title, reserving for the first of the highest class the title of Emperor. . . .
>
> 13. Every month there shall be a general examination before the parish priest and the teachers to determine the advancement the pupils may have made . . . in writing, reading, arithmetic, Christian doctrine, etc. . . .
>
> 14. From pupils studying the alphabet, the syllabary, and reading, the teacher shall hear four lessons a day, two in the morning and two in the afternoon. . . .
>
> 15. Pupils in arithmetic or counting shall solve two problems a day, write one or two exercises, read two lessons and receive instructions in Christian doctrine once in the afternoon. . . .
>
> 17. The teachers shall instruct their pupils how to assist at Mass. . . .
>
> 18. When the Procession of the Rosary leaves the parish church and passes through the streets, the teachers shall attend with their pupils, no exception being allowed. . . .

1. What subjects were taught in the school at St. Augustine? _____
_____

2. How was this school different from the one you attend? _____
_____

3. Give three examples that show that religion was an important subject at the school.
_____

CHAPTER REVIEW: CRITICAL THINKING

The Spanish colonies began to change after the American Revolution. There were more people from cultures other than Spanish and Native American in some of the territories. Many brought their own customs and cultures. Spanish culture also began to influence the behavior and customs of some of the people who came from the United States.

1. Give some examples from this chapter of how people from different cultures learned from
one another. _____
_____

2. Give some examples of how Spanish culture affected the culture of the United States.
_____

UNIT 3 REVIEW

Summary of the Unit

A few of the important events and facts presented in Unit 3 are listed below. Write these events and facts in your notebook and add three more.

1. Spain ruled Louisiana from 1762 to 1800. It was the only part of Spain's North American empire with mostly French settlers.
2. Eighteenth-century Spanish explorers sailed up the northwest coast and blazed new trails to California. As they did they opened new ports and started new communities.
3. The mission system brought Spanish culture to the New World.
4. Spain and its colonies helped the 13 colonies during the American Revolution by supplying money and military assistance.
5. After the American Revolution, the Spanish returned to Florida, and cattle ranching became an important part of life in the Southwest.

Understanding What You Have Read

Choose each correct answer and write the letter in the space provided.

_____ 1. One of the greatest poets of New Spain (Mexico) was
   a. Father Junípero Serra.
   b. Sor Juana Inés de la Cruz.
   c. Vicente Manuel de Zéspedes.

_____ 2. Malaspina was sent to look for
   a. gold and slaves.
   b. a glacier.
   c. a northwest passage.

_____ 3. The Spanish colonies were
   a. mostly based on Native American culture.
   b. unwilling to accept new foods.
   c. a mixture of Spanish and Native American cultures.

_____ 4. Most of the money the Cubans gave to the American Revolution came from
   a. the king of Spain.
   b. Cuba's governor.
   c. the wealthy women of Havana.

_____ 5. Bernardo de Gálvez helped the 13 colonies during the American Revolution by
   a. driving the British out of the Mississippi Valley and the Gulf of Mexico.
   b. fighting alongside Americans in the 13 colonies.
   c. training the Continental army.

_____ 6. The people who settled in Florida in 1784 were
   a. mostly from Spain.
   b. from many parts of Europe.
   c. mostly from Louisiana.

_____ 7. Louisiana was sold to the United States by
   a. Cuba.   b. France.   c. Spain.

_____ 8. Laureano de Torres y Ayala was an important governor of
   a. Florida.   b. Louisiana.   c. Texas.

Building Your Vocabulary

Write the correct word next to the best phrase that describes it. Not all choices will be used.

ranchero	cabildo	criollo	presidio	mulato
mestizo	peninsular	pueblo	vaquero	creole

_____ 1. person born in the New World of Spanish parents

_____ 2. person who was born in Spain and came to America

_____ 3. person of mixed Spanish and Native American background

_____ 4. council used to help the governor

_____ 5. a fort

_____ 6. owner of a large ranch

_____ 7. Mexican-American cowboy

_____ 8. small town or community

_____ 9. person of mixed European and African background

Developing Ideas and Skills—Using a Time Line

Study the time line. Then answer the questions, by writing the letter of the correct time period in the space provided.

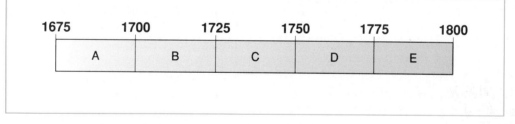

_____ 1. Eusebio Kino began to explore Arizona and build missions there.

_____ 2. Malaspina reached the coast of Alaska.

_____ 3. Gálvez defeated the British in an important battle.

_____ 4. The wealthy women of Havana collected their jewels to help support the American Revolution.

_____ 5. Antonio de Ulloa became the first Spanish governor of Louisiana.

Making History Live

1. Use the school library or public library to write a report on one of the people mentioned in the unit who is of most interest to you.
2. Prepare a "television news story" about one event in this unit. Make your own maps or illustrations to go with the story.
3. Make a list of 25 English words that come from Spanish words. Use a dictionary that will help you find the origin of words now used in English. Some dictionaries will tell you at what date the word entered the English language.

Chapter 15 THE EARLY 19th CENTURY

AIM: Who were the Hispanics in the United States in the early 19th century? What were some of the reasons for the War of 1812?

1. In the early 19th century there was no commonly used word for people who spoke Spanish but did not come from Spain. Today, many people use the words **Hispanic** or **Latino** to describe Spanish-speaking people or people with Spanish traditions. English-speaking people of North America are sometimes called **Anglo-Saxons** or **Anglos**. These words mean "English," but many of these people do not have English family backgrounds. They may have German, French, or other backgrounds. However, Anglos speak English. Likewise, some Hispanics may not have Spanish family backgrounds. But they may speak Spanish or have some Spanish traditions.

2. As early as 1654, a group of 23 **Sephardic Jews** left Brazil and landed in New Amsterdam—now New York City. The word *Sephardic* comes from the Hebrew word for Spain. They were descendants of Jews who had been forced to leave Spain by Ferdinand and Isabella in 1492. They spoke **Ladino**, a kind of Spanish. However, many had Spanish names. Spain at that time did not consider them Spanish because they refused to become Christian.

▲ The Battle of New Orleans is pictured above. Did the War of 1812 result in the United States's gaining control of all of Florida? Explain.

By the early 19th century only a small number of Sephardic Jews lived in the United States.

3. By 1800, many *criollos*, *mulatos*, and *mestizos* had moved to new places in the Americas. A few came to the United States. Some of these United States citizens married people who were not of Spanish **heritage**, or tradition. Their children often kept their Spanish heritage.

4. In 1812, the United States and Great Britain were at war again. This time Spain was on Great Britain's side. The United States was fighting for the right to use the seas freely. The United States was also fighting against the practice of **impressing** Americans. The British had been impressing American sailors, that is, forcing them to serve on British ships.

5. Among those who fought for the United States were people of Spanish background. For example, Jorge Ferragut offered to serve his adopted country. He had fought in the American Revolution. Ferragut was in his fifties and had an injured arm. Yet he fought for a short time on the Mississippi River, but his poor health forced him to stop. His young son David Farragut, an American sailor, fought the British off the coast of Chile.

6. The United States hoped to gain both Canada and Florida in the war. The United States managed to take the area around Mobile (at that time part of Florida) early in 1812. The British were supposed to have left Florida in 1783. However, Pensacola had remained a British base.

7. In December 1814, the United States and Britain signed the Treaty of Ghent. The treaty ended the war, but neither side gained anything. News of the treaty did not reach the British or United States armies in time to stop the Battle of New Orleans. On January 8, 1815, General Andrew Jackson won the Battle of New Orleans. His troops included people of Spanish descent who lived in New Orleans as well as people from Santo Domingo. More than 2,000 British soldiers died. The United States had only 21 dead or wounded. Jackson became a popular hero.

A. Answer the following questions.

1. What is one of the main ideas in *paragraph 1?* _____
   _____

2. How would you define the word *Hispanic?* _____
   _____
   _____

3. What were the goals of the United States during the War of 1812? _____
   _____
   _____

B. In each of the sentences that follow, the underlined words make the sentence true or false. If the sentence is true, write **T** in the blank before it. If it is false, write the word or words that would make the sentence true.

_____ 1. During the War of 1812, Spain was on <u>Great Britain's</u> side.

_____ 2. The Sephardic Jews who landed in New Amsterdam in 1654 came from <u>Brazil</u>.

_____ 3. During the War of 1812, the United States wanted to gain Canada and <u>Mexico</u>.

_____ 4. The treaty that ended the War of 1812 was signed <u>after</u> Andrew Jackson won the Battle of New Orleans.

_____ 5. The British lost <u>more</u> soldiers than the Americans in the Battle of New Orleans.

Daily Life

Popular Dancing. One of the popular dances of the early 19th century was the **fandango.** The lively music for this dance probably came from the Spanish colonies in the Americas in the late 1600s. The dance and music spread to Spain. The music for the fandango was usually performed with guitars and castanets.

▲ The fandango was a popular dance in many of the Spanish colonies.

1. Where did the popular fandango begin? _____

2. Use your school library or public library to find out where one of the following 20th-century dances (and its dance music) began and in what countries it was most popular: tango, rumba, mambo, cha–cha, salsa. Write a one-paragraph report on it.

Spotlight on People

Jorge Ferragut. Jorge Ferragut was born in 1755 on the island of Minorca, off the coast of Spain. Most of the people on Minorca spoke Spanish. However, when Ferragut was born, Minorca was ruled by Great Britain. Ferragut left Minorca when he was 17 and became a **merchant marine** captain. The merchant marine is made up of the trading ships of a country. He sailed his own ship in the Caribbean Sea, the Atlantic Ocean, and the Gulf of Mexico.

The American Revolution gave Ferragut a new opportunity. He did not like the British. That was because in 1713 the British had taken over the island of Minorca from Spain. Ferragut became a first lieutenant and then a ship's captain in South Carolina's navy. During the American Revolution, he fought the British in Savannah and was captured at Charleston.

After Ferragut regained his freedom in a prisoner exchange, he joined the Continental army. He fought in the battles of Cowpens and Wilmington. He was wounded in the arm, which became paralyzed. By the end of the war, Ferragut had become a major in the cavalry.

After the American Revolution, Ferragut moved to Tennessee. There he married American-born Elisabeth Shine.

George Farragut, as he was now known, moved his family to New Orleans for greater opportunity. He built armed ships for the navy to defend New Orleans. Then he became a captain of an armed ship.

Farragut patrolled the Mississippi River. Even though he was 57 when the War of 1812 began, he led his ship on United States missions. Before long, his injured arm and illness made it impossible for him to continue fighting. Years later, George Farragut's son David would become the first United States admiral.

Recalling the Facts

Choose each correct answer and write the letter in the space provided.

_____ 1. Jorge Ferragut was born in
   a. Havana.
   b. Britain.
   c. Minorca.

_____ 2. *Before* the American Revolution, Ferragut was
   a. a captain in the merchant marine.
   b. a shipbuilder.
   c. a member of South Carolina's navy.

_____ 3. Before he joined the Continental army, Ferragut
   a. fought on the British side.
   b. joined South Carolina's navy.
   c. fought at Cowpens.

_____ 4. During the **American** Revolution, Jorge **Ferragut's**
   a. boat was sunk.
   b. loyalty was to Britain.
   c. arm was badly injured.

_____ 5. George Farragut fought in the War of 1812
   a. just after his son was born.
   b. when he was 57.
   c. soon after he was married.

_____ 6. George Farragut was
   a. the husband of a major writer.
   b. the son of a naval officer.
   c. the father of the first U. S. admiral.

The Arts and Technology

Arts and Handicrafts. In the 1800s, many arts and handicrafts developed in New Mexico. One important industry was the making of religious items for churches and homes. People known as **santeros** carved religious statues and scenes. The statues of saints are known as **santos**. The religious scenes are called **retablos**. Today many of these religious items are highly valued by art collectors.

Jewelry making was another important art. Skilled workers made gold and silver jewelry. Often the jewelry had lacy designs known as **filigree**. The art of making filigree jewelry in the styles popular in New Mexico came from Spain and from the **Moors** who had lived in Spain.

▲ This filigree jewelry was made in New Mexico. Filigree jewelry has a carefully crafted and delicate design with open spaces between gold or silver.

1. Why do you think religious art was important in New Mexico?_____

_____

2. How does this style of jewelry made in New Mexico show a Spanish heritage?

_____

_____

CHAPTER REVIEW: CRITICAL THINKING

The War of 1812 was fought between the United States and **Great** Britain, but it was related to wars in Europe between Great Britain and France. This war is sometimes called the "Second American Revolution" because Americans proved the country could survive. The war gave Americans a feeling of pride in their country.

1. How do Jorge Ferragut's actions show he was proud to be an American? _____

_____

2. What do you think might have happened if the United States had lost the war against Great

Britain? Explain. _____

_____

THE UNITED STATES ACQUIRES FLORIDA

1. The United States wanted Florida. In 1803, Thomas Jefferson tried to buy West Florida as part of the Louisiana Purchase. He did not succeed. Some Americans, however, claimed that West Florida was part of the Louisiana Purchase.

2. In 1810, a group of Americans moved into West Florida. They captured the Spanish fort at Baton Rouge. The Americans declared the independence of the "Republic of West Florida." In October 1810, President James Madison claimed that the United States controlled West Florida from the Mississippi River to the Perdido River. Spain objected, but Spain was fighting a war in Europe and could not fight the United States. In 1813, the United States took over the rest of West Florida after capturing the Spanish fort at Mobile. It seemed just a matter of time before Spain would be forced to give up East Florida too.

3. For many years, East Florida had been a

▲ The Spanish fire a cannon salute before lowering the Spanish flag and leaving the fort in St. Augustine to the Americans.

hiding place for pirates and smugglers. Runaway slaves escaped across the border from the United States into East Florida. The Seminole Native Americans used the border areas as bases from which to make raids into the United States. The Seminoles had moved from the United States into Florida but tried to get their land back. In 1817, the United States government gave the war hero Andrew Jackson orders allowing him to chase the Seminoles across the border into Spanish territory.

4. In 1818, General Andrew Jackson attacked the Seminoles who had crossed into Georgia. He followed them back into Florida and captured the Spanish forts of St. Marks and Pensacola. Jackson's forces captured two Seminole leaders and two British fur traders, accused of arming the Seminoles. The Seminole leaders were hanged without a trial. The two British subjects were executed after their trials. Jackson also removed the Spanish governor.

5. Jackson's actions were against the law. However, most of the American public praised his deeds. Great Britain did not protest, but Spain did. United States Secretary of State John Quincy Adams blamed Spain. He accused the Spanish of encouraging the Seminoles to attack. Adams demanded that Spain either control the Seminoles or give up Florida.

6. Spain was having trouble with its other American colonies and so was willing to give up Florida. Adams worked out the Adams-Onís Treaty with Luis de Onís, the Spanish official in Washington. The United States signed the treaty in 1819. Spain signed it in 1821. The treaty said that both East and West Florida belonged to the United States. It drew up a western border between the Louisiana Territory and Spanish territory. Spain gave up its claim to the land in Oregon. In return, the United States gave up any claim to Texas. The United States **agreed** to pay over $5 million that Spain owed United States citizens. The United States also agreed to honor all land grants made before January 1, 1818.

A. In each of the sentences that follow, the underlined word or words make the sentence true or false. If the sentence is true, write **T** in the blank before it. If it is false, write the word or words in the blank that will make it true.

_____ 1. West Florida <u>was not</u> included in the Louisiana Purchase.

_____ 2. <u>Slaves</u> took the fort at Baton Rouge and declared the independence of the Republic of West Florida.

_____ 3. The fort the United States captured at Mobile was in <u>East</u> Florida.

_____ 4. General Andrew Jackson pursued the <u>Seminoles</u> into Florida.

_____ 5. According to the Adams-Onís Treaty, the United States agreed to give up its claim to <u>Louisiana</u>.

B. Place the events below in the correct order by writing the numbers 1 through 5 in the blanks.

_____ a. General Andrew Jackson enters East Florida and captures two Spanish forts.

_____ b. Americans declare the independence of the Republic of West Florida.

_____ c. The United States buys Louisiana.

_____ d. Spain signs the Adams-Onís Treaty.

_____ e. The United States takes over the rest of West Florida.

Building Geography Skills

Study the map. Then answer the questions.

1. When did the United States acquire the *western* section of West Florida?

_____

2. What river formed the border between East and West Florida?

_____

3. When did the United States acquire St. Augustine?

_____

4, From what country did the United States gain Florida?

_____

The United States Gains Florida from Spain

Mississippi River
Pearl River
WEST FLORIDA
Baton Rouge
New Orleans
Mobile
Pensacola
St. Marks
St. Augustine
EAST FLORIDA

GULF OF MEXICO

☐ Acquired in 1810
☐ Acquired in 1813
☐ Acquired in 1819

0 50 100 Miles
0 50 100 Kilometers

Joseph Hernández. Joseph Hernández was born in Florida at the end of the 18th century. His parents were Minorcans who settled in Florida in 1768.

When Florida became part of the United States in 1819, Joseph Hernández swore allegiance to his new country. In a few years, he became the first Hispanic in Congress.

Under the rule of the United States, Hernández, a plantation owner, served on St. Augustine's city council. He then became mayor of St. Augustine.

In 1822, when Florida was a territory, Hernández became its first delegate to the U.S. Congress. He could speak on issues, but he could not vote. Two years later, Hernández was elected president of the legislative council of Florida.

During the Second Seminole War, Joseph Hernández became a brigadier general and raised an army of volunteers. The Second Seminole War was fought from 1835 until 1842. In January 1836, Hernández fought a group of Seminoles at a plantation near St. Augustine. Several months later, he captured Seminole Chief Phillip and the chief's followers.

Shortly after that, a Seminole prisoner led the general to a Seminole camp in the swamps. There he captured two Seminole chiefs. In a few short months, General Hernández had taken five important leaders prisoner.

Two other outstanding Native American leaders, Osceola and Coa Hadjo, wanted to discuss peace. Under orders from Major General Thomas Jesup, General Hernández ignored their truce flag and captured the chiefs in 1837. By 1842, most of the Seminoles finally agreed to move west. A few of them, however, settled in the Everglades, a large area of marshes and swamps in southern Florida. Hernández ran unsuccessfully for the U.S. Senate in 1845, then moved to Florida.

Recalling the Facts

Choose each correct answer and write the letter in the space provided.

_____ 1. Joseph Hernández was born in
   a. the United States.
   b. Minorca.
   c. Florida.

_____ 2. When the United States acquired Florida, Hernández
   a. swore allegiance to the United States.
   b. fought against the Americans.
   c. moved to Spanish territory.

_____ 3. Hernández's first public job under the United States was
   a. member of the city council.
   b. mayor of St. Augustine.
   c. territorial delegate from Florida to Congress.

_____ 4. During the Second Seminole War, Hernández
   a. told the government it was wrong.
   b. sided with the Seminoles.
   c. raised an army to fight.

_____ 5. After capturing five Seminole leaders, Hernández
   a. captured two more.
   b. resigned as general.
   c. proposed a peace treaty.

_____ 6. Hernández captured Osceola and Coa Hadjo by
   a. surprising them near St. Augustine.
   b. ignoring a truce flag.
   c. showing a truce flag.

The Arts and Technology

The González-Alvarez House. The oldest house in St. Augustine, Florida, is the González-Alvarez House. It was built between 1702 and 1727. The house and its furniture reflect the mixture of different cultures of the owners. For example, some of the windows are made of small pieces of glass held together by lead that had been melted and then hardened. Such leaded glass windows were used in England in large homes in the 17th and 18th centuries. The building is now a National Historic Landmark and a museum for people to visit.

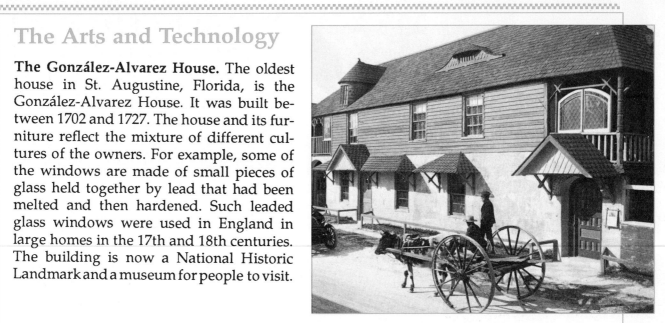

1. The cultures of what countries would you expect to find represented in the González-Álvarez House? _____

    _____

2. How does this house's architecture differ from that of the buildings shown on pages 35 and 37? _____

    _____

3. List three differences between this house and the buildings that are people's homes in your community. _____

    _____

CHAPTER REVIEW: CRITICAL THINKING

When you read about almost any issue, you learn **different points of view.** To understand history, it is important to understand why people act and think the way they do. In the early 19th century, many United States citizens believed the United States had a right to own Florida. The Spanish, as well as the British and the Seminoles, also wanted Florida.

1. What argument might a United States citizen of the early 19th century have given for making Florida a United States territory? _____

    _____

2. What argument might a 19th-century Spanish subject have given to show that Florida should be ruled by Spain? _____

    _____

3. What argument might a Seminole have given for controlling land in Florida? _____

    _____

    _____

Chapter 17 MEXICO AND ITS INDEPENDENCE

AIMS: How did Mexico gain its independence? Why did the United States issue the Monroe Doctrine?

1. By 1790, Mexico and other **Latin American** colonies had been under European control for about 300 years. Those colonists, like the American colonists, finally decided that they wanted freedom from European control. A series of revolutions took place throughout Latin America from 1791 to 1824. Mexico's revolution began in 1810.

2. The first step toward independence in Mexico was begun by Father Miguel Hidalgo y Costilla. He was a *criollo* priest in the town of Dolores. He led a rebellion against the Spanish. His actions inspired other Mexicans to rebel in other regions. In 1811, Hidalgo was captured and killed by Spanish troops, but his spirit of revolution lived on.

3. José María Morelos, also a priest, continued the Mexican War of Independence. He organized a trained army and won many victories. In 1813, he declared Mexico independent, and he started a new government. The *criollos* did not support Morelos, however. By 1815, Morelos was captured and shot.

4. For the next five years, the revolution slowed down. Only small groups of rebels led by Vicente Guerrero continued the fight. In 1820 Agustín de Iturbide was sent by the **royalists**, supporters of the Spanish king, to stop Guerrero. Instead Iturbide joined Guerrero. Both leaders had so much support that little fighting took place. By the end of 1821 Mexico became independent of Spain.

5. Once Mexico was independent there was disagreement over who should rule the country. There was also disagreement over how Mexico should be ruled. Iturbide took over the Mexican government by force in 1822. He was declared Emperor Agustín I. Within 10 months the Mexican people were dissatisfied with him. General Antonio López de Santa Anna seized power from Iturbide in 1823. Mexico became an independent republic in 1824.

6. During this time, leaders in the United States were interested in the struggles for independence. They also were concerned about changes in Europe. Russia, Austria, and Prussia were strong European countries. They were ruled by absolute monarchs. All three countries had agreed to end all forms of representative government in Europe. Government leaders in the United States worried that the European leaders might want to end representative government in the Americas also.

7. The **Monroe Doctrine** was written as a clear warning to the European nations. On December 2, 1823, President James Monroe delivered the Monroe Doctrine to the United States Congress. In it the United States declared that it would not allow new colonies to be created on the American continents. It said that existing colonies could not change their boundaries. It also said that the United States would protect all independent nations of the Western Hemisphere from European threats.

▲ The woman in this early 19th-century painting represents Mexico. Father Hidalgo is shown crowning her with a laurel wreath that stands for victory. What does the broken chain stand for?

Place the events below in the correct order by writing the numbers 1 through 6 in the blanks.

_____ Iturbide takes control of Mexico.

_____ Morelos organizes a strong revolutionary army.

_____ Father Hidalgo leads a rebellion that begins the Mexican War of Independence.

_____ Guerrero and Iturbide join forces to work for Mexico's independence.

_____ Santa Anna removes Iturbide from power.

_____ Mexico is declared independent in 1821.

Building Geography Skills

Study the map. Then answer the questions.

1. Which country on the map was the first to gain its independence?

   _____

2. Which country was first in the 19th century to gain independence: Mexico, Chile, or Cuba?

   _____

3. What is the largest non-Spanish colony to gain its independence in South America? _____

4. José de San Martín trained an army in Argentina and crossed the Andes Mountains into Chile with Bernardo O'Higgins. They freed Chile in what year? _____

5. In what direction did San Martín sail from Chile to Peru to help free part of Peru? _____

6. Simón Bolívar fought Spanish forces for many years. He freed an area that is now Colombia, Panama, and Venezuela. Bolívar and Antonio José de Sucre freed Ecuador in 1822. In what year did they free Peru? _____

7. In what year did Bolivia declare its independence?

   _____

Early 19th Century Independence for Colonies in the Americas

MEXICO 1821
CUBA 1898
HAITI 1804
DOMINICAN REPUBLIC 1821
HONDURAS 1821
NICARAGUA 1821, 1838
GUATEMALA 1821
EL SALVADOR 1821
COSTA RICA 1821
PANAMA 1821, 1903
VENEZUELA 1811, 1821, 1830
COLOMBIA 1819
ECUADOR 1822, 1830
PERU 1824
BRAZIL 1822
BOLIVIA 1825
PARAGUAY 1811
CHILE 1818
ARGENTINA 1816
URUGUAY 1828

ATLANTIC OCEAN

PACIFIC OCEAN

0   500   1000 Miles
0 500 1000 Kilometers

Former Spanish colonies
Note: Map shows today's names and boundaries.

N W E S

Father Miguel Hidalgo. On September 16, 1810, Father Miguel Hidalgo y Costilla rang the church bell in the Mexican town of Dolores. He cried out, "Long live Our Lady of Guadalupe, down with bad government, down with the Spaniards!" His call is known as the *Grito de Dolores*, the "cry of Dolores." That cry marks the beginning of the Mexican fight for independence. He hoped to liberate Mexico from Spain, free the slaves, and return land to the Native Americans.

Hidalgo was born in Mexico in 1753. He graduated from the University of Mexico. He became a parish priest, but he soon found himself in trouble with the Spanish officials. To improve the lives of the Native Americans in his parish, he had set up some factories. The Spanish did not permit the Mexican Native Americans to work at these factories. Because of this, Hidalgo was tried for heresy, or a belief in something the Church said was false.

The priest joined a group that wanted to free Mexico and its people from Spanish rule. Hidalgo, who was nearly 60 years old, gathered an army of Native Americans and captured the towns of Guanajuato and Guadalajara. A religious feeling marked his actions. On his banner was the figure of Our Lady of Guadalupe, the patron saint of Mexico.

Father Hidalgo, with an army of about 80,000, attacked government forces near Mexico City. His army won their first battle. Then they had to retreat. María Josefa Ortiz de Domínguez, another hero of the Mexican Revolution, was able to warn Father Hidalgo that he would be arrested. Father Hidalgo and a few leaders tried to escape. Hidalgo was captured and shot.

Recalling the Facts

Choose each correct answer and write the letter in the space provided.

_____ 1. Hidalgo began the Mexican fight for independence by
a. building a factory.
b. ringing a bell.
c. waving a religious banner.

_____ 2. Hidalgo hoped to
a. free the slaves.
b. get more land for the Creoles.
c. get a better job for himself.

_____ 3. María Josefa Ortiz de Domínguez
a. helped the Spanish.
b. warned Father Hidalgo that he would be arrested.
c. forced the Native Americans off their land.

_____ 4. The *Grito de Dolores* was
a. The name of Father Hidalgo's church bell.
b. a nickname for Father Hidalgo.
c. Father Hidalgo's cry for freedom.

_____ 5. The army Father Hidalgo led near Mexico City numbered
a. only a few hundred.
b. a few thousand.
c. about 80,000.

Using Primary Sources

The Monroe Doctrine. In 1823, President James Monroe made a speech to Congress. His message became known as the Monroe Doctrine. The United States said it would protect countries in the Western Hemisphere from European threats. However, Mexico and other Latin American countries resented the Monroe Doctrine and the growing power of the United States. The Latin American countries had given the United States the nickname "the Colossus of the North." By the mid-1800s, Mexico would find itself in a struggle with "the Colossus of the North."

> The American continents, by the free and independent condition which they have assumed [taken on] and maintained [kept], are . . . not to be considered as subjects for future colonization by any European powers. . . .
>
> The citizens of the United States cherish sentiments [feelings] . . . in favor of the liberty and happiness of their fellow-men on [the European] side of the Atlantic. . . . It is only when our rights are invaded or seriously menaced [threatened] that we . . . make preparations for our defense. With the movements in this hemisphere [the Americas] we are of necessity more immediately connected. . . .We . . . declare that we should consider any attempt on their [the Europeans'] part to extend [spread] their system to any portion of this hemisphere as dangerous to our peace and safety . . . .
>
> But with the governments who have declared their independence and maintained it, and whose independence we have . . . acknowledged [recognized], we could not view any interposition [interference] for the purpose of oppressing them, or controlling . . . their destiny . . . in any other light than as . . . an unfriendly disposition [act] toward the United States . . . .

1. What phrase says that the countries of Europe should not try to make new colonies in Latin America? _____

2. How does Monroe say the United States will feel about any attempt to place new European colonies in Latin America? _____

CHAPTER REVIEW: CRITICAL THINKING

The nations of Latin America were fighting for independence at the same time that the United States was trying to gain Florida from Spain. Spain did not want the United States to recognize the independence of Spain's former colonies. Florida became a United States territory in 1821. Despite Spain's wishes, the United States recognized the independence of Colombia and Mexico in 1822, Chile and Argentina in 1823, Brazil and the Central American states in 1824, and Peru in 1826.

1. Why didn't Spain want the United States to recognize the independence of the Latin American countries? _____

_____

2. Do you think the United States should have recognized their independence sooner or later? Explain. _____

_____

Chapter 18 TEXAS AND INDEPENDENCE

AIMS: Which people wanted Texas to be an independent republic? What were their reasons?

1. When Mexico became independent from Spain in 1821, Anglos had already begun to move into Texas. Some had permission to do so. They were *empresarios.* They were given large amounts of land. In return, they brought large groups of settlers. The settlers agreed to become Roman Catholics, to conduct business in Spanish, and to obey Mexican laws. The most famous *empresario* was Stephen Austin. He brought about 300 settlers to Texas beginning in 1821. By 1832, Austin's settlement had 8,000 people. There were about 22,000 other Anglos in Texas.

2. Conflicts between the new settlers and the Mexican government grew. Many Anglos were cotton farmers from the southern United States. They brought their slaves with them. In 1829, Mexico declared that slavery was against the law. The new settlers did not like this law. The settlers were also unhappy because Mexican law did not guarantee trial by jury. There was no bill of rights.

3. By 1830, Anglos greatly outnumbered Mexicans in Texas. The settlers from the United States wanted to live under their own laws. Mexico reminded them that they were citizens of Mexico. In 1830, Mexico declared that Anglo immigration to Texas was supposed to end. That also angered settlers. Stephen Austin went to Mexico City in 1832 to ask for more self-government for Texas. He was refused. Austin was thrown in jail for urging the settlers to form a state government. After his release, Austin agreed with those who wanted independence.

4. In 1833, Antonio López de Santa Anna became president of Mexico. He centralized the power of government so that people in Texas and other Mexican states would have little say in government.

5. Fighting began in 1835. Mexican troops tried to take a cannon from the Texan town of Gonzales. Then Texan rebels attacked and captured San Antonio in late 1835. Santa Anna led a large army to stop the rebels at San Antonio. A group of rebels gathered at a mission called the Alamo. Many of these people had been in Texas for a short time. Many of them were not Texans but Americans who wanted to separate Texas from Mexico. With them were nine Hispanic Texans led by Captain Juan Seguín. Santa Anna defeated the rebels at the Alamo in March 1836. Santa Anna went on to Goliad, where he fought the Texans, who finally surrendered. Santa Anna had 330 prisoners shot. He burned towns and crops.

6. However, Santa Anna was soon to be defeated. In April 1836, Sam Houston led the Texan forces in a surprise attack against Santa Anna's troops at the San Jacinto River. The Texans shouted, "Remember the Alamo! Remember Goliad!" The Texans won the battle and captured Santa Anna. They forced Santa Anna to give up Texas. A few weeks earlier, on March 2, 1836, the Anglos and a few Mexicans had declared Texas an independent republic. The Mexican government refused to recognize the new Republic of Texas, but the United States did.

▲ Mexican troops attack the Alamo. Who won the 12-day battle, the Mexicans or the Texans?

Answer each of the following questions in the space provided.

1. What did Anglo settlers agree to do when they moved to Mexican-controlled Texas in the 1820s? _____

2. What is the main idea of *paragraph 2*? _____
_____

3. What were *empresarios* expected to do in return for the large amounts of land they received?
_____

4. Who was Mexico's ruler during the fight for Texas independence? _____
_____

5. Who was the leader of the Hispanics fighting against the Mexicans at the Alamo?
_____

6. In what year did Texas become an independent republic? _____

Building Geography Skills

Study the map. Then answer the questions.

1. What were two of the Texan victories in the Texas War for Independence?

_____

_____

2. What were two Texan defeats in this war?

_____

_____

3. What countries bordered the Republic of Texas?

_____

_____

4. What countries claimed the land between the Rio Grande and the Nueces River from 1836 to 1845?

_____

_____

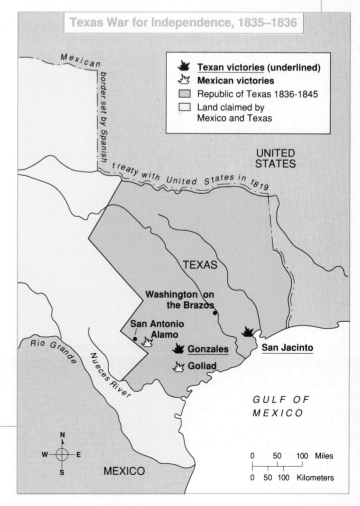

Texas War for Independence, 1835–1836

- ★ Texan victories (underlined)
- ⚔ Mexican victories
- ▢ Republic of Texas 1836-1845
- ▢ Land claimed by Mexico and Texas

Mexican border set by Spanish treaty with United States in 1819

UNITED STATES

TEXAS

Washington on the Brazos

San Antonio
Alamo

Rio Grande

Nueces River

Gonzales

Goliad

San Jacinto

GULF OF MEXICO

MEXICO

0 50 100 Miles
0 50 100 Kilometers

Lorenzo de Zavala. After a long career serving Mexico, Lorenzo de Zavala became a leader in the struggle for Texas independence. He became the first vice president of the new republic.

Lorenzo de Zavala was born in 1788 in the southeastern part of Mexico. He studied to be a priest but changed his mind. For a while, he represented his region in the Spanish parliament in Spain.

Zavala helped write the Mexican Constitution of 1824. This constitution created the Mexican Federal Union. Texas was one of that union's provinces. Zavala served as a senator and as a state governor in Mexico, then as Mexico's treasury minister. Later, Zavala represented Mexico in France.

In 1829, the Mexican government gave Zavala a land grant in Texas. Zavala opposed President Santa Anna's policies, so he moved to Texas in 1835. Zavala signed the Texas Declaration of Independence. He also designed the first flag adopted by the Republic of Texas.

Zavala was elected vice president of the Republic of Texas in March 1836. However, poor health soon forced him to resign. He died at home later that year.

Lorenzo de Zavala wrote several books on Mexican history. His granddaughter, Adina Emilia de Zavala, fought to save historic sites in Texas. She helped keep part of the Alamo from being destroyed.

Recalling the Facts

Choose each correct answer and write the letter in the space provided.

_____ 1. Lorenzo de Zavala was born in
   a. Spain. **b.** Texas. **c.** Mexico.

_____ 2. Zavala went to Spain as
   a. minister of the treasury.
   b. writer of the Constitution.
   c. representative from his region.

_____ 3. Under the Mexican Constitution of 1824, Texas was
   a. a province of Mexico.
   b. an independent republic.
   c. part of the United States.

_____ 4. Zavala got a land grant from
   a. the state of Texas.
   b. the Republic of Texas.
   c. the government of Mexico.

_____ 5. Zavala signed
   a. a document that made Santa Anna the dictator of Mexico.
   b. the Texas Declaration of Independence.
   c. the United States Declaration of Independence.

_____ 6. Historic sites in Texas, including part of the Alamo, were saved for us to visit by
   a. Santa Anna.
   b. Adina Emilia de Zavala.
   c. Lorenzo de Zavala.

The Arts and Technology

The Alamo. The Alamo has become a symbol of the Texas fight for independence. Here, after a 12-day battle, the Mexican forces of several thousand defeated fewer than 200 defenders of the Alamo in 1836.

The Alamo, named after the Spanish word for cottonwood tree, was not built as a presidio, or fort. It was built as the Spanish mission of San Antonio de Valero. On page 31, you studied a 1720s map of the area. A hurricane destroyed the mission, but it was rebuilt in 1727. Later in the 1700s, Spanish soldiers turned it into a military post and barracks, or rooms to live in. However, the Alamo was not built for defense. The walls were not high enough to offer a great deal of protection.

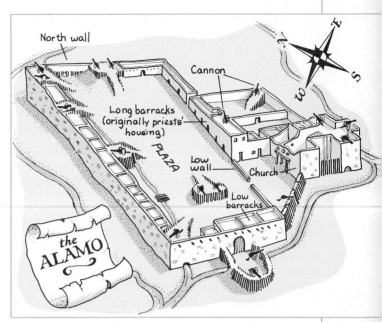

1. What building in the Alamo reveals that it was built as a mission, not as a presidio?

   _____

2. What were the soldiers' long barracks used for before the rooms were turned into

   barracks in the 1700s? _____

   _____

3. The buildings were built of stone. In other parts of the Spanish colonies in North America what building materials were used in mission architecture? _____

   _____

CHAPTER REVIEW: CRITICAL THINKING

Often there are several solutions to a problem. It is important to **know the alternatives** before acting. In the same way, when studying history, you can better understand why people acted as they did by learning about the alternatives they had.

1. What were some of the alternatives Anglo settlers in Texas had besides revolting? If you had been an Anglo settler in the 1830s in Texas what would you have done? Why?

   _____

   _____

2. Suppose you had been the ruler of Mexico in the 1830s. What were some of the alternatives to using military force to keep Texas a part of Mexico? What would you have done? Why?

   _____

   _____

Chapter 19 THE MEXICAN WAR

AIMS: What led to the war with Mexico? How were Hispanics in the United States territories treated after the war?

1. After Texas gained its independence from Mexico in 1836, the Anglos promised the Mexicans in Texas that they would be equal citizens. Hispanics living in Texas had a year to choose to remain or move to Mexico. Those who stayed were promised the same rights as others. Their lives and property were to be respected. However, not all Anglos kept that promise. Some Anglos tried to force the Mexicans to move south of the Rio Grande. Even Juan Seguín, who had fought for Texas's independence, was forced to move south.

2. For about 10 years, Texas grew as an independent republic. Armed disputes between Texas and Mexico continued. In 1845, Texas was admitted to the United States of America as the 28th state. Mexico broke off relations with the United States soon after Texas became a state. Then the United States and Mexico disagreed over Texas's border. Mexico claimed that the southern border of Texas was marked by the Nueces River. The Texans and the United States said the border was along the Rio Grande, which is farther to the south.

3. In April 1846, Mexican troops crossed the Rio Grande. They turned back a small American force under Major General Zachary Taylor. The American troops had entered the disputed border area. In May, the United States declared war on Mexico. The reasons the United States declared war went far beyond the defeat at the Rio Grande. The United States leaders wanted the disputed land and wanted Mexico to sell it to the United States.

4. The Mexican War lasted until early 1848. Major General Taylor led a United States army across the Rio Grande and defeated the Mexicans at Monterrey and Buena Vista. In the Southwest, General Stephen W. Kearny led a small United States army westward from Santa Fe to California. When Kearny reached California he found that a group of Americans under Captain John Frémont had revolted against Mexico. They had set up their own government called the Bear Flag Republic. Frémont had been helped by an American fleet in the Pacific. In March 1847, General Winfield Scott led another army that landed near the port of Veracruz. By May, Scott had captured both Veracruz and Mexico City.

5. Finally in February of 1848 the Mexican War ended with the signing of the **Treaty of Guadalupe Hidalgo.** In that treaty Mexico reluctantly agreed to give Mexican lands to the United States. These lands were called the **Mexican Cession.** The lands included what is today California, Nevada, Utah, and parts of New Mexico, Arizona, Wyoming, and Colorado. In exchange for the land the United States paid the Mexican government $10 million. The treaty also protected the property and rights of Mexicans who stayed in Texas.

6. Many of the Mexicans who stayed in the Southwest quickly learned that the Treaty of Guadalupe Hidalgo could not change people's attitudes. They lost much of their land to the Anglos. They were not given fair trials. Some Mexicans were even shot or lynched.

▲ Americans attack the Castillo de Chapultepec near Mexico City. Young military cadets called Los Niños, became heroes trying to defend the castle.

In each of the sentences that follow, the underlined word or words make the sentence true or false. If the sentence is true, write **T** in the blank before it. If it is false, write the word or words that would make it true.

_____ 1. After Texas became a republic, <u>all</u> Mexicans in Texas were treated fairly and equally.

_____ 2. In 1845 Texas was <u>refused admission</u> as a state in the United States.

_____ 3. Mexico was <u>glad</u> that Texas became a state in the United States.

_____ 4. Mexico claimed that its border with Texas should be at the <u>Nueces River</u>.

_____ 5. In April 1846 American troops defeated the Mexicans in a battle at the <u>Rio Grande</u>.

_____ 6. The United States declared war on Mexico in <u>1848</u>.

_____ 7. The <u>Treaty of Guadalupe Hidalgo</u> ended the Mexican War.

_____ 8. The Mexicans were <u>glad</u> to give up the lands that today include California, Nevada, Utah, and parts of New Mexico, Arizona, Wyoming, and Colorado for $10 million.

_____ 9. <u>John Frémont</u> fought for Texas independence but then moved south of the Rio Grande under pressure from Anglos.

Daily Life

The Spanish introduced many new foods into the Americas. The Native Americans had eaten meats such as turkey, deer, and buffalo before the Spanish came. The Spanish brought cattle, sheep, goats, pigs, and chickens to the Americas. They also brought wheat and rice to grow in America. The Spanish learned about harvesting corn, beans, and squash from Native Americans. A stone called a **mano** was used to grind corn by hand on another stone called a **metate**.

As the Spanish influence in the Americas grew, so did the spread of foods. For example, crops such as tomatoes and chili peppers spread from Mexico into the United States. Many new styles of cooking developed from the new variety of foods and cultures.

▲ What were the stone tools this woman used to grind corn into flour?

What are some of the Hispanic influences on foods you eat today? _____

_____

Spotlight on People

Juan Seguín. Juan Seguín was born in San Antonio in 1806. Seguín was a good friend of Stephen Austin. At the age of 18, Juan Seguín was elected *alcalde*, or mayor, of San Antonio.

Juan Seguín supported the Texan independence movement. When the Texans rebelled against Mexico, Seguín became a captain in the Texas cavalry. He fought at the Alamo, but he was sent through enemy lines to get help before the final Mexican attack. Seguín continued to fight for independence. He reached the rank of lieutenant colonel. While he was off fighting, his wife, Josefa, trained more soldiers.

After the Texas War for Independence, Seguín was put in command of San Antonio. He had to protect San Antonio from attacks by the Mexican forces. He also had to protect Mexicans in Texas who were being mistreated by the Anglos. Finally Seguín was forced to resign because of pressure from the Anglos. The Anglos charged him with treason. Concerned about his safety, Seguín moved to Nuevo Laredo, just south of the Rio Grande.

The Mexicans put Seguín in prison. However, Santa Anna freed him when Seguín agreed to join the Mexican army. The Mexican army tried twice to retake Texas. But those attempts failed. By 1848 Seguín was allowed to return to Texas. He lived there until his death.

Recalling the Facts

Choose each correct answer and write the letter in the space provided.

_____ 1. Juan Seguín was born in
  a. Mexico City.
  b. Nuevo Laredo.
  c. San Antonio.

_____ 2. At 18, Seguín became
  a. a captain in the army.
  b. governor of Texas.
  c. mayor of San Antonio.

_____ 3. During the Texas War for Independence, Seguín
  a. fought on the Texan side.
  b. fought on the Mexican side.
  c. refused to take part.

_____ 4. Seguín did not die at the Alamo because
  a. he was never there.
  b. he went for help.
  c. his side won the battle.

_____ 5. Josefa Seguín
  a. drilled her husband's troops.
  b. refused to help her husband.
  c. served as mayor when her husband was absent.

_____ 6. After the Texas war, Seguín moved to Nuevo Laredo because
  a. he was worried about his safety.
  b. the Anglos ordered him to go.
  c. the land was better there.

Using Primary Sources

The Treaty of Guadalupe Hidalgo. The treaty was signed on February 2, 1848, ending the Mexican War. The United States Congress ratified the treaty on May 30, 1848.

> ARTICLE VIII Mexicans now established [living] in territories previously belonging to Mexico, and which remain for the future within the limits of the United States . . . shall be free to continue where they now reside [live], or to remove [move] at any time to the Mexican republic, retaining [keeping] the property which they possess . . . or disposing [selling the property] and removing the proceeds [money gained from a sale] wherever they please, without their being subject . . . to any contribution, tax, or charge whatever. . . .
>
> ARTICLE IX [These people are guaranteed] the enjoyment of all the rights of citizens of the United States according to the principles of the Constitution; and in the meantime shall be maintained and protected in the free enjoyment of their liberty and property, and . . . in the free exercise of their religion. . . .

What rights did the treaty give Mexicans then living within the United States?

_____

_____

CHAPTER REVIEW: CRITICAL THINKING

Many Americans in the 1840s began to speak of America's **manifest destiny**—or *natural right*—to take over territory in Texas, California, and elsewhere. They believed that the will of God or of fate intended the United States to rule others in what they believed was a better form of government.

1. How would the idea of manifest destiny help to explain the war with Mexico?_____

_____

_____

2. Suppose you were a Mexican in the 1840s. How might you have reacted to the idea of the

   United States's manifest destiny? Explain. _____

_____

_____

Chapter 20

THE CIVIL WAR

1. The Civil War took place in the United States from 1861 to 1865. Nearly 10,000 Hispanics fought in the war. Some fought for the Union, others for the Confederacy. Some of them fought in all-Hispanic regiments led by Hispanic officers. Others were integrated into the regular army or into volunteer units.

2. José Francisco Chaves fought in the Union army. During the Civil War, he became a lieutenant colonel. He fought in the Battle of Glorieta Pass in March 1862. In that battle, Chaves helped the Union army recapture the area around Albuquerque and Santa Fe from the Confederates.

3. Santos Benavides was born in Laredo, Texas, in 1827. He was elected mayor of that city in 1857. He joined the Confederate army and held the highest rank among Hispanic-American officers in the South. His unit, called the "Benavides Regiment," was stationed near Laredo, Texas. In March 1864, Benavides and his regiment went to Brownsville, Texas. There they drove back the attacking forces.

4. Cuban-born Loretta Janet Velásquez enlisted in the Confederate army in 1860. She was disguised as a man. She fought in the battles of Bull Run and Ball's Bluff in Virginia. She also fought at Fort Donelson in Tennessee. In 1862 the army discovered Velásquez's disguise and discharged her. She managed to re-enlist, and she fought at Shiloh in April 1862. Her disguise was discovered again, and she was discharged from the army again. She then became a successful spy for the South.

5. Another Cuban-born soldier in the Civil War was Federico Fernández Cavada. Captain Cavada served as an engineer in the Union army. Later he was placed in charge of hot-air balloons that spied on the enemy. Cavada took part in the battles of Antietam, Fredericksburg, and Gettysburg. The Confederates captured him at the Battle of Gettysburg. They sent him to Libby Prison in Richmond, Virginia. After his release, he wrote a book on life in that Confederate prison.

6. The most famous Hispanic American in the Civil War was David Farragut. Farragut began his naval career by serving as an apprentice in the United States Navy. When the Civil War broke out, he joined the Union navy.

7. In 1862 Farragut was ordered to capture New Orleans and take control of the Mississippi River. New Orleans had two strong Confederate forts. First Farragut bombarded those forts. Then he sailed past them at night and overcame the small fleet of Confederate ships. He captured New Orleans on April 25, 1862. Farragut continued up the Mississippi River. He took several key Confederate forts. His successes helped cut important Confederate supply and communication routes. They also helped General Ulysses S. Grant win the Battle of Vicksburg.

▲ After David Farragut's victory at Mobile Bay he gained the rank of admiral of the navy. There were Hispanic heroes on both the Union and Confederate sides.

A. Write the names of the persons below next to the statement that each might have made.

Santos Benavides   Federico Fernández Cavada   David Farragut
José Francisco Chaves   Loretta Janet Velásquez

_____   1. I fought for the Union army at Glorieta Pass.

_____   2. My regiment saved Brownsville from a Union attack.

_____   3. I was born in Cuba and served the South, first as a soldier, then as a spy.

_____   4. I was an army engineer, and I fought in major battles before I was captured by the Confederates.

_____   5. As a naval commander for the Union, I captured New Orleans.

B. In each of the sentences that follow, the underlined word makes the sentence true or false. If the sentence is true, write **T** in the blank before it. If it is false, write the word or words that make the sentence true.

_____   1. A few <u>hundred</u> Hispanic Americans fought in the Civil War.

_____   2. Hispanic Americans fought on <u>both</u> sides in the Civil War.

_____   3. Loretta Janet Velásquez was a spy for the <u>Union</u>.

_____   4. Hot-air balloons were used during the Civil War for <u>battle</u>.

_____   5. Farragut successfully cut off the <u>Confederates</u> from their supply lines along the Mississippi River.

Linking Past to Present

Read the following information about aerial surveillance. Then answer the questions that follow.

In the 19th century, balloons were used for **aerial surveillance,** or watching from the air. The balloons that Federico Fernández Cavada worked with were captive balloons. These balloons were attached to the ground by ropes. The balloons were used mainly to see where Confederate troops were and which way they were moving.

Today, armies use satellites and aircraft to survey the enemy and help plan attacks. They sometimes use balloons to gather weather information and to trick enemy radar.

▲ This Civil War balloon was used for gathering information on the enemy's military position.

1. What was the main purpose of the balloons Cavada worked with? _____

_____

2. How is aerial surveillance done today? _____

_____

David G. Farragut. David Farragut was born James Farragut in 1801 near Knoxville, Tennessee. He changed his first name to David in honor of David Porter. Porter was a naval captain who adopted Farragut and trained him aboard ship.

Farragut began training to become a great naval captain at the age of 9. When he was 13 years old, he served on the USS *Essex*. There he saw action in the War of 1812. In his twenties, he fought pirates in the West Indies. He was also in the attack on Veracruz, Mexico, in 1822. This was during Mexico's fight to become a republic.

Farragut is probably most well-remembered for his capture of Mobile, Alabama, during the Civil War. In August 1864, Farragut brought a group of wooden ships and four ironclad submarines to Mobile Bay. The bay was filled with Confederate torpedoes, ready to explode with the slightest bump. The first of Farragut's vessels hit a torpedo and exploded. After that explosion, Farragut's wooden ship took the lead. Farragut has been quoted as shouting, "Damn the torpedos! Full steam ahead!" The rest of his fleet entered the bay safely. In the bay, Farragut's ships and the Confederate ironclad CSS *Tennessee* battled fiercely. Finally the CSS *Tennessee* had to surrender. Mobile was soon captured.

The United States Congress created the rank of admiral of the navy for Farragut. It was in honor of his outstanding service during the Civil War.

Recalling the Facts

Choose each correct answer and write the letter in the space provided.

_____ 1. David Farragut was born in
   a. Tennessee.
   b. Texas.
   c. Kentucky.

_____ 2. Farragut first served in the United States navy when he was
   a. 9.   b. 13.   c. 18.

_____ 3. In his twenties, Farragut
   a. fought in Mexico.
   b. fought in the War of 1812.
   c. left the navy.

_____ 4. One of Farragut's well-known naval battles was in
   a. the Gulf of Mexico.
   b. the Chesapeake Bay.
   c. Mobile Bay.

_____ 5. For his service during the Civil War, Farragut became a naval
   a. colonel.
   b. captain.
   c. admiral.

Using Primary Sources

Life in a Prisoner-of-War Camp. While he was in the Libby Prison, Federico Fernández Cavada wrote and drew pictures on any paper he could find. He wrote on the margins of old newspapers and on scraps of paper. He hid these notes in his shoes and socks. After he was freed in 1864, Cavada's writings were published in a book called *Libby Life*. It described the harsh conditions in the Confederate prison.

▲ This photo of Libby Prison, in Richmond, Virginia, was taken in 1864.

> There are some [prisoners] who cannot sleep. They are thinking of the camp, of home, and of friends. They are quarreling with the fortune of war. They are longing for the termination [end] of a loathsome and hateful captivity, which has only just begun.

1. What might have made prison life "loathsome and hateful"? _____
   _____

2. Why would the thoughts of the prisoners keep them from sleeping? _____
   _____

3. Many soldiers died in Civil War prisoner-of-war camps. What conditions might have
   led to some deaths? _____.
   _____

CHAPTER REVIEW: CRITICAL THINKING

During the Civil War, Hispanic Americans as well as other citizens of the United States took opposite sides. It was a war in which brothers and friends fought each other because of the sides they chose. Some Hispanic Americans chose the Union side. Others chose the Confederate side. Their choices were based on where they lived or what they believed.

1. Why, do you think, did Hispanic Americans fight in the Civil War? _____
   _____

2. How were the actions of the Hispanic Americans during the Civil War like those of Americans of other backgrounds? _____
   _____

UNIT 4 REVIEW

Summary of the Unit

A few of the important events and facts presented in Unit 4 are listed below. Write these events and facts in your notebook and add three more.

1. Hispanics from many places moved to the United States and the Spanish empire.
2. From 1810 to 1819, the United States invaded Florida and gradually acquired it.
3. In the early 1800s, the colonies of Spanish America fought for and won their independence from Spain.
4. Settlers from the United States moved into Texas, outnumbered the Mexicans, and fought for and won the independence of Texas.
5. After Texas became a state, Mexico and the United States fought a war in which Mexico lost about a third of its land to the United States.
6. Hispanic Americans fought on both sides of the Civil War.

Understanding What You Have Read

Choose each correct answer and write the letter in the space provided.

_____ 1. In the War of 1812, the United States wanted to acquire
    a. Mexico and Texas.
    b. New Orleans and Louisiana.
    c. Florida and Canada.

_____ 2. The First Seminole War began when
    a. Andrew Jackson followed Native Americans into Florida.
    b. Osceola declared war against the United States.
    c. Joseph Hernández became governor of Florida.

_____ 3. After Mexico became independent,
    a. it fought Spain for possession of Texas and California.
    b. it passed a law allowing slavery.
    c. California and Texas became Mexican territory.

_____ 4. One reason many Americans in Texas did not like Mexican law was
    a. it did not allow slavery.
    b. it permitted slavery.
    c. Americans could not own land.

_____ 5. After the Treaty of Guadalupe Hidalgo,
    a. Americans respected the rights of Mexicans who remained.
    b. Mexican rights were often ignored.
    c. Mexico gained more land.

_____ 6. The first United States admiral was
    a. Federico Fernández Cavada, who was born in Cuba.
    b. David Porter, an American.
    c. David Farragut, whose father was Spanish.

Building Your Vocabulary

Write a definition for each term.

1. *empresario:* _____

2. Latino: _____

3. Ladino: _____

4. *retablo:* _____

5. merchant marine: _____

6. heritage: _____

Developing Ideas and Skills—Using Time Lines

Study the time line. Then write the letter of the correct time period in the space next to each event.

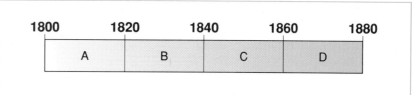

1800	1820	1840	1860	1880
A	B	C	D	

_____ 1. Texas becomes a United States state.

_____ 2. Mexico becomes independent.

_____ 3. Father Hidalgo gives the *Grito de Dolores*.

_____ 4. Texas declares itself an independent republic.

_____ 5. Mexico and the United States sign the Treaty of Guadalupe Hidalgo.

_____ 6. President Monroe announces the Monroe Doctrine.

_____ 7. The United States annexes West Florida.

Building Map Skills

Study the map. Then answer the questions.

1. What states or parts of states make up the Mexican Cession, gained from Mexico in 1848?

   _____

   _____

   _____

   _____

   _____

The United States Gains Mexican Lands

WYOMING

NEVADA

NEBRASKA

UTAH

CALIFORNIA

COLORADO

KANSAS

ARIZONA

NEW MEXICO

OKLAHOMA

TEXAS

M E X I C O

☐ State of Texas, 1845
☐ Mexican Cession, 1848
☐ Land purchased from Texas by the United States, 1850
☐ Gadsden Purchase, 1853
☐ State of Texas after 1850

0   200   Miles
0   200   Kilometers

2. In 1853, the United States forced Mexico to sell it land for $10 million. This was called the **Gadsden Purchase,** land valuable for its natural resources. Americans also planned to build a railroad across it. Parts of what states make up the Gadsden Purchase of 1853?

   _____

   _____

Making History Live

1. Find a cookbook of recipes from the Southwest. Go through some recipes and decide which ingredients were Native American and which were Spanish. Try some of the recipes.
2. Choose one of the following people: Simon Bolívar, David Farragut, María Josefa Ortiz, José de San Martín. Make up an "album" of a major event in that person's life.
3. Study the flags of Florida, Texas, New Mexico, Arizona, and California. Look for clues about the history of each state in its modern and older flags. Write a brief report.

Glossary

adelantado governor (p. 20)

adobe a bricklike building material made of sun-dried earth and straw (p. 27)

aerial surveillance watching the earth's surface from balloons or aircraft (p. 85)

Anglo a North American whose home language is English (p. 64)

Anglo-Saxon a person descended from the white Anglo-Saxon tribes who conquered England in the 5th century (p. 64)

bronco a wild horse (p. 59)

cabildo a town council (p. 40)

caravel a type of ship used in the 1400s (p. 5)

chaps short name for the leather leggings worn by cowboys (p. 59)

chaparreras leather leggings worn by cowboys (p. 59)

conquistadores leaders of the Spanish conquest of America (p. 6)

corral fenced area for holding cattle or horses (p. 59)

Creole originally a European born in the New World (p. 47)

criollo originally a person born in the Americas whose parents came from Spain (p. 46)

duty tax (p. 38)

empresario a person who brought settlers to Mexican-ruled Texas in exchange for land (p. 76)

encomendero an early Spanish settler owning a large land grant (p. 14)

encomienda a large grant of land and the people living on it given to early Spanish settlers in the New World (p. 14)

fandango a popular dance in many Spanish colonies (p. 65)

filigree a lacy design on fine jewelry (p. 67)

front an area of fighting in a war (p. 57)

Gadsden Purchase lands purchased by the United States from Mexico in 1853. Includes parts of present-day Arizona and New Mexico. (p. 89)

Grito de Dolores "Cry of Dolores." Father Hidalgo's call for Mexico's independence. (p. 74)

heritage a person's customs and traditions (p. 64)

hidalgo a Spanish gentleman. Member of Spain's lower nobility. (p. 28)

Hispanic a person whose language and traditions come from Spanish-speaking countries (p. 64)

impress to force a person into naval service (p. 64)

la reata American Spanish term for a lariat or lasso used for roping cattle (p. 59)

Ladino a language of Spanish and Hebrew words spoken by Sephardic Jews (p. 64)

lariat a cowboy's tool for roping cattle (p. 59)

Latin America lands in Mexico, Central and South America, and parts of the Caribbean that were once ruled by Spain, France, or Portugal (p. 72)

Latino a Spanish-speaking person from Mexico, Central or South America, or the Caribbean (p. 64)

maize a grain also known as corn (p. 46)

manifest destiny American belief in the 1840s that the United States should expand across the North American continent and Caribbean region (p. 83)

mano upper stone used in grinding corn (p. 81)

marqués a Spanish noble (p. 28)

merchant marine trading ship of a country (p. 66)

mestizo a person of mixed Spanish and Native American origins (p. 46)

metate lower stone used in grinding corn (p. 81)

Mexican Cession Mexican lands won in 1848 by the United States in the Mexican War. Includes present-day California, Nevada, Utah, and parts of New Mexico, Arizona, Wyoming, and Colorado. (p. 80)

mission a religious center built to teach Christianity and western ways to Native Americans (p. 14)

missionary a person who works to spread a religion (p. 15)

Monroe Doctrine an American policy begun in 1823 to keep the Western Hemisphere free of outside influences (p. 72)

Moors Muslims who ruled southern Spain until 1492 (p. 67)

nao a type of sailing ship in the 1400s (p. 5)

New World the Western Hemisphere lands of North, Central, and South America (p. 2)

peninsular (singular), **peninsulares** (plural) people born in Spain to Spanish parents (p. 46)

plaza an open area or public square in a city or town (p. 27)

presidio Spanish military fort (p. 28)

pueblo (1) Spanish word meaning "town" (p. 32); (2) name given by early Spanish settlers to apartmentlike Native American villages in present day Arizona and New Mexico (p. 17)

ranchero rancher or owner of a large land area (p. 32)

rancho a ranch or large land area often used to raise cattle or sheep (p. 32)

reata a cowboy's tool for roping cattle (p. 59)

rebozo long shawl worn mainly by rich Mexican women (p. 45)

retablo religious picture hung in a church (p. 67)

royalist supporter of the Spanish king (p. 72)

santero Hispanic-American maker of religious statues and paintings (p. 67)

santos saints (p. 67)

sarape colorful woolen blanket worn over the shoulders. Also spelled serape. (p. 45)

Sephardic Jew a Jew whose ancestors lived in Spain before 1492 (p. 64)

sombrero a big, wide-brimmed hat (p. 59)

strait narrow waterway connecting two large bodies of water (p. 42)

Treaty of Guadalupe Hidalgo 1848 treaty giving much of northern Mexico to the United States (p. 80)

tribute a kind of tax, paid in corn, cloth, or work (p. 24)

vaquero a cowboy (p. 32)

Index